CW01261762

DONALD CAMPBELL

300+ **A SPEED ODYSSEY**

HIS LIFE WITH BLUEBIRD

DAVID de LARA

The History Press

ACKNOWLEDGEMENTS

Gina Campbell, Tonia Bern-Campbell, Ken and Lewis Norris, Alfredo Fernandez, Maurice James, Robin Brown, Ken Burvill, Christine Bairstow, Brian Caddy, Bill Coley and Mary Coley, Jim Coughlan, Sandy Doggart, Clive Gill, Ray Govier, Graham Gunsen, Geoff and Mary Hallawell, Keith Harrison, Ray Hewertson, John and Heather Fenn, Geoff Holden, Mike Fuller, Lorne Jacobs, Tony James, John Norris, Ken Norris' PA Barbara, Robbie and Liz Robinson, Angus Tuck, Tony Stuchbury, K7 Club, National Motor Museum at Beaulieu, Steve Milne, Molinare, Windermere Motor Boat Racing Club, Ken Reaks, Joyce Villa, Jean Wales née Campbell, Don Wales, Vicky Slowe, Ruskin Museum, Longines Watch Company Francillon SA., Ken and Dave Warby,

Special thanks to the 'Burberry's for their participation:

Steve Holter, Neil Sheppard and Don Stevens.
Big thank you to Christine Bairstow for her kindness and enthusiasm.

Photo credits:

Leo Villa, Donald Campbell, Bob Murphy, Robin Grosvenor, Geoff Hallawell, Madame Yevonde, *Evening Mail*, Richard Noble (Thrust Cars Ltd), *Westmorland Gazette*.

Karl Rogerson: p 186, 190, 191, 192, 193, 194, 195, 198.
Eddie Whitham: p 186, p 190, p 198
Tony James: p 181, p 184, p 185, p 186
Cover: L. Villa and E. Whitham

Photo archives and collections:

Leo Villa, Neil Sheppard, Tonia Bern-Campbell, Ruskin Museum, Geoff Holden, Martin Summers, Mike Varndell, Gina Campbell, John Norris, Ken Norris, BP, Longines of Switzerland, Shell Group, Goodyear.

Design: Martin Squires (*sketchbooktravels.com*)
Cover design: The History Press
Technical drawings, Bluebird speed tables and illustrations: Mick Hill.
Arty shots of Coniston Water: Tony Stuchbury.
Painting of Donald Campbell: Gloria Avila (*gloria-avila.com*)

Photo credits Barmera and Dumbleyung:

Leo Villa, Bernie McNamara, Jean Pearse, Brian Caddy, Dot Collins, John Ward, Tom Brown, Ron Lloyd, Joan Ward, McPherson and Tom Brown.

Photo credits Coniston 1966/67:

Eddie Whitham, Karl Rogerson, 16 mm clip courtesy of Neil Sheppard, Tony James, Michael Ockenden, Leo Villa, Ken Norris archive, Leo Villa archive, Bill Vanryne and Mirrorpix.

First published 2016

The History Press
The Mill, Brimscombe Port
Stroud, Gloucestershire, GL5 2QG
www.thehistorypress.co.uk

© David de Lara, 2016

The right of David de Lara to be identified as the Author of this work has been asserted in accordance with the Copyright, Designs and Patents Act 1988.

All rights reserved. No part of this book may be reprinted or reproduced or utilised in any form or by any electronic, mechanical or other means, now known or hereafter invented, including photocopying and recording, or in any information storage or retrieval system, without the permission in writing from the Publishers.

British Library Cataloguing in Publication Data.
A catalogue record for this book is available from the British Library.

ISBN 978 0 7509 7008 2
Printed in India

Contents

Donald Campbell was my hero by Ken Warby MBE	4
Foreword by Gina Campbell	6
Don from Surrey by David de Lara	9
No more the Bloomsbury-puff by Steve Holter	9
Legend by Neil Sheppard	9
My Speed King by Tonia Bern-Campbell	9
Eternal Challenge (1921-1948)	10
Altar of Speed (1949-1955)	38
Fast and Loose (1955-1959)	82
How Long a Mile (1960-1963)	122
Past the Point of no Return (1964-1967)	150
Of Men and Machines	202
Spirit of Australia II by Dave Warby	203
Campbell-Norris 7	204
Chronocinégines	208
Unlimited Brothers Norris by Donald Stevens & Mike Pepper	210
My Friend Ken Norris by Steven Holter	212
Jetstar	214
One man and his dream – 50 years on by Christine Bairstow	216
Peter Carr by Donald Stevens	218
Leo Villa OBE	219
Bluebird Speed Tables	220
Index	224

Donald Campbell was my hero

On 8th October 1978, Australian Ken Warby, in his jet-powered, unlimited class hydroplane, Spirit of Australia, took the World Water Speed Record for the second time at 317.58 mph (275.97 knots or 511.11 km/h) on Blowering Dam Lake, New South Wales, Australia. With a peak speed of 345 mph on the return run he lives to share his adventure. The magic 300 mark has been exceeded twice by Ken and once fatally by Donald Campbell in 1967.

As a young boy I was fascinated by the record breakers of the day and made many models of boats, it was the early drawings that I saw of Bluebird K7 which really got my attention. All it took was to build a 12-inch version out of balsa wood, a small Jetex 50 rocket engine, and I was on my way to the local pond. It was an event that changed my life.

I followed the adventures of Donald Campbell closely and was in awe of his achievements, telling my family much to their amusement that I wanted to follow in his footsteps. My first race boat was built at the age of 15, a 10-foot ply hull with a 4-cylinder Ford Prefect motor. It was a disaster but it got me started on a lifelong adventure. Joining the local powerboat club, looking at the fast boats of the day and asking lots of questions over many years, I built and raced quite a number of very quick boats.

The water speed record was never far from my mind. In 1969 I finally sat down at the kitchen table with a sheet of drawing paper and a pencil and the rest is history. The story of speed on water is littered with death and destruction. As boats were fitted with jet engines, speeds increased dramatically and so did the death rate. Any driver attempting the record must ask himself the question, how badly do I want it, as the chances of living through it are not good and will only get worse as speeds rise.

Breaking the World Water Speed Record has become one of the most dangerous endeavours known to man. I made my peace with my maker before I ever made my runs and left it up to him for the result. Mind you, a good well-designed and built boat does help the odds.

Donald Campbell faced those challenges many times and was always aware of what the results could be. Anybody that is not totally aware of the danger should not be in the cockpit. Over the past years I have visited Coniston on a number of occasions to pay my respects to Donald at his grave, meet members of his team, and even help raise funds for the Bluebird restoration. The most memorable trip I experienced was meeting with Leo Villa at his home, just before his passing. Leo and I had been exchanging cassette tapes during the period of my record runs. I would let him know how my runs went and he would make comments as well as give me encouragement. Leo referred to Spirit of Australia as my homemade boat. Leo was a wonderful, gentle man and I am honoured to have known him.

The Donald Campbell story is one of courage and perseverance. He was and is a true hero. RIP Donald.

Ken Warby MBE, 2016

Donald Campbell CBE with Bluebird K7, Coniston Water, 1956.

Foreword

Being born into the Clan Campbell is without doubt the most privileged, humbling and amazing position, as Sir Malcolm my grandfather and Donald my father were real life superheroes within their fields and national heroes of their time. They both achieved enormous goals within world, land and water speed record-breaking through many decades during the 20th century, taking record speeds up in leaps and bounds, risking their lives and limbs, all in the sheer pursuit of attaining something that had never been achieved before ... their own 'blue bird of happiness'.

My dad used to say to me: 'unless you strive for the top and reach it you'll never make anything of your life. In fact you'll be a waste of space.' I thought this was a bit harsh and overbearing, but it was what his own father had said to him ... words like: you're a bloody clod boy and always will be! ... So one is forever judged by results only, and anyone who has competed in any form of sport knows that it is impossible to be Number One all of the time.

David asked me what made DC tick. That made me think hard, because it would be much too easy to say that he was driven by this massive desire to be and attain this, this and this and all the other records. My thoughts and instinct, bearing in mind I was only 17 when my father was killed, are that apart from wanting 'to be the fastest', to be The World Record Holder etc. and a great desire to emulate and prove to be accepted as the son of the great Sir Malcolm Campbell, was that record-breaking became his business. It was one of his sources of income, it employed people, it was innovative, it was his livelihood, it kept the 'wolf from the door'. Now this isn't to say it was all about financial reward, as there was the massive public interest and kudos that he attained which opened all sorts of other doors. Imagine if my father and grandfather for that matter, were at the height of their careers in 2016 they would be splashed across the headlines all day, every day, every movement caught on camera, every good thing and bad catalogued and dissected; there would be talk shows and interviews galore, it would be non-stop media activity. Fame in their eras was fame for achievement and for outstanding success, not for what people are famous for today, in some cases just their good-looks! These men were very, very, iconic and achieved the accolades they deserved in the way expressed in those days ... hence we are talking and writing about them today.

I believe that history has treated them very kindly and given them their well-earned status, their followers and their adorers. I personally have to thank all those involved for keeping my father's life and achievements up there in the public's eye. Were they 'before their time'? I think not: they were in the times when technology relied upon human endeavour, success or failure, with the ultimate sacrifice. Today a computer can do it all for you but not then.

In a very strange way, despite all my father's amazing record-breaking successes, he's remembered most for the visually dramatic and mind-blowing way he died in 1967 on Coniston Water at the helm of Bluebird K7. You know, should he have lived out a long happy life in an armchair reading the papers till 90 years old, when he died there would have been a few very nice column inches in the papers announcing his death and acknowledgements of his previous life but as it is now he's got this amazing following of enthusiasts, engineers, clubs and organisations that commemorate at every opportunity his life and achievements. The books and TV documentaries all bear testament to this ... wonderful.

Gina Campbell, 2016

7

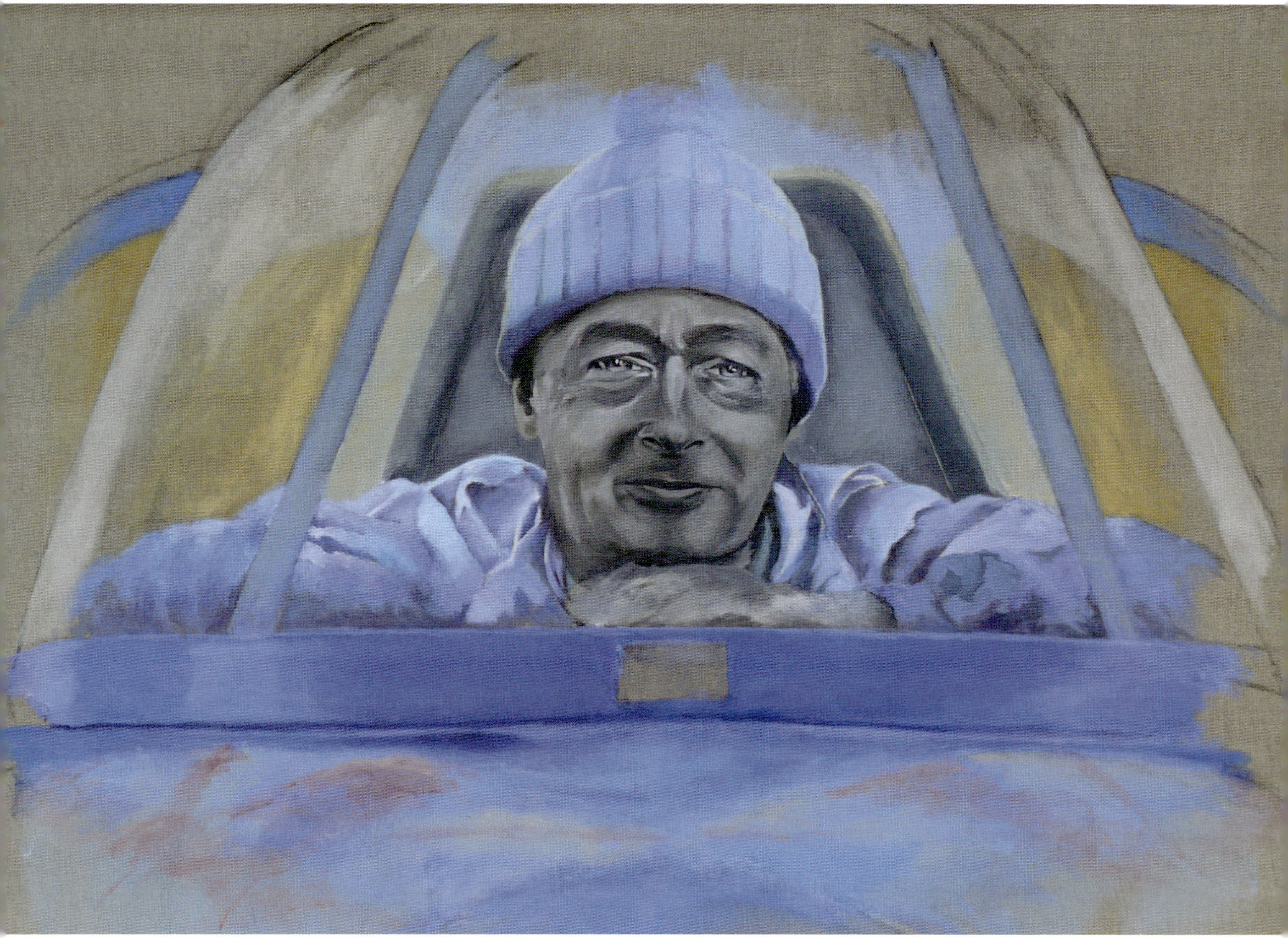

Don from Surrey

Donald Campbell was a true blue British original, born in a country known for creating its share of colourful and unique individuals. He stands apart for his level of eccentricity, thirst for speed and lust for passion. He was a brave man, with a streak of the daredevil and test pilot. A 1930s public school bourgeois, he had a playboy attitude and the matinee-idol looks to go with it. Between 1955 and 1967 he held the record for the fastest man on water. Since 1964 he remains the only record breaker to hold and take both the land and water speed records in the same year. The Double.

This album has the advantage of having had the assistance of Donald's daughter. Whilst he never kept private diaries, Gina gave me access to his letters, memos, notes, a big box of photos and unfinished manuscripts which make up the early years in the book. The other voices are from interviews recorded for the film *Remembering Donald* and feature the Bluebird designers, Ken and Lew Norris, Robbie Robinson and Donald's widow, Tonia. In addition to interviews, the other adventures are drawn from Leo Villa's recollections, commentaries and discussions recorded on C-90 cassettes with Donald, Ken Warby, Kevin Desmond and Tony Gray. *Donald Campbell 300+ A Speed Odyssey: His Life with Bluebird* is a storyboard of the main events in Donald Campbell's life between 1921 and 1967, animated by those that were there or close to him.

David de Lara

No more the Bloomsbury-puff!

Donald Campbell could get things done. His two Bluebirds are testimony: They were the most advanced vehicles of their time. Bluebird CN7 was of monocoque construction, before it became commonplace in Grand Prix racing. The Bluebird K7 boat was built using a method never before envisaged and resembled a fighter aircraft rather than a hydroplane.

In 1966, when the Bluebird K7 boat was converted from its Beryl installation, to the lighter, more powerful Orpheus, it was no simple nut-and-bolt job. There exist nearly as many calculations, drawings and schemes for the conversion as for the original 1955 design.

Suggestions were made that the 300+ attempt was slap-dash that Donald's spectacular failure was due to the little thought that had gone into the conversion: Bluebird's trim had to be altered with the addition of lead ingots in the stern, shaped in biscuit tin lids by the freezing lakeside; there was the collapse of the air intake ducting, and many alterations to the anti-splash deflectors, yet Grand Prix Lotus mechanics in the 1980s could be seen, in the pits, filing down the front uprights of a Lotus 80 racing car because they had been found to be rubbing on the wheels. This type of incident was commonplace in that époque with this type of on-the-edge engineering; but with Donald Campbell it was presented as a great failing.

Steve Holter

Legend

On 4th January 1967, Donald Campbell was piloting his jet-propelled Bluebird in search of his eighth World Water Speed Record when suddenly and inexplicably the boat took off, climbed into the air and somersaulted before impacting the concrete-like surface. Campbell was killed instantly.

His death left behind a mystery: who was he really, and why was he at Coniston in 1966?

Donald Campbell loved life and lived it well. He was light of heart and optimistic of nature, but behind the public façade of the speed king laid a complex character – proud and vulnerable, anxious about his place in the world. He was also tired. He had been doing the impossible for more than 15 years – carrying on his father's role in an age when logic told him everything was against him. He wanted the support to carry on achieving for Britain, but towards the end that support had failed. Donald Campbell, 50 years after the event, will always be remembered for what he became at the point Bluebird left the surface of Coniston Water: a legend.

Neil Sheppard

My Speed King

My beloved Donald. I can still hear his laughter and his jokes. I can see the pride in his eyes when he spoke of his country and its people. I melt when I remember his kindness to animals and I hurt when I think of the small boy trying to please his father and how I adored that naughty grin when he winked at me. I never felt more at home than when in his arms and I admired his determination to bring glory to Britain. He never thought he would become a legendary hero and there are many other things he never knew ... I would keep his name up there and carry it with pride; after all I was a very lucky woman. In those precious eight years I received more and felt more than most women in a lifetime. The girl from Knokke-le-Zoute had shared the life of the most exciting, fun-loving, daring Speed King. I had received a beautiful love and a sensational outlook on life. No, I had no right to cry any more ...

Tonia Bern-Campbell

ETERNAL CHALLENGE
1921-1948

Striving for speed records is very much like exploring, the faster man travels the more difficulties he encounters, the more he is determined to overcome and understand them; and as he proceeds, stage by stage, so gradually he penetrates farther into the unknown. It becomes something of a disease in the blood, which feeds on inclination and atmosphere.

Donald Campbell CBE

Malcolm Campbell

I was born Donald Malcolm Campbell on 21st March 1921, and until the outbreak of World War II in 1939, the ambitions and achievements of my father were by far the most dominant and influential forces in my life. Dad and I were the greatest of friends and as close in companionship as any father and son can be.

Povey Cross

I grew up in the electric atmosphere of the unceasing striving for higher speeds and greater speed records, it had settled firmly over our family home, Povey Cross in Surrey. Throughout my childhood, my father, Sir Malcolm Campbell, was breaking and re-establishing the World Land Speed Record with the Blue Bird car on an annual basis. By the time I was 18 he had held this nine times and the World's Water Speed Record four times, a record he still held the day he died on New Year's Eve, 1948.

Malcolm Campbell named his racing car Blue Bird and the name passed from car to car, from race track to speed record breaking, from land to water, from father to son. Over the passage of time, as each speed record succeeded another, each one became a milestone of human advancement, a book perhaps without an end, a book in which a man has something to write about his struggles, successes and failures on ascending the mountain of evolution.

Life is an eternal challenge, a variant of Maeterlinck's theme that the blue bird of happiness is by the side of each and every one of us, always within reach, if pursued to catch and possess, is beyond our grasp.

Each one of us can only go so far, for the mountain of creation has no summit as it leads to the stars and must be climbed. There is no regress for man, he may pause momentarily, but there is no going back on the path of life. Once you start something you are already past the point of no return.

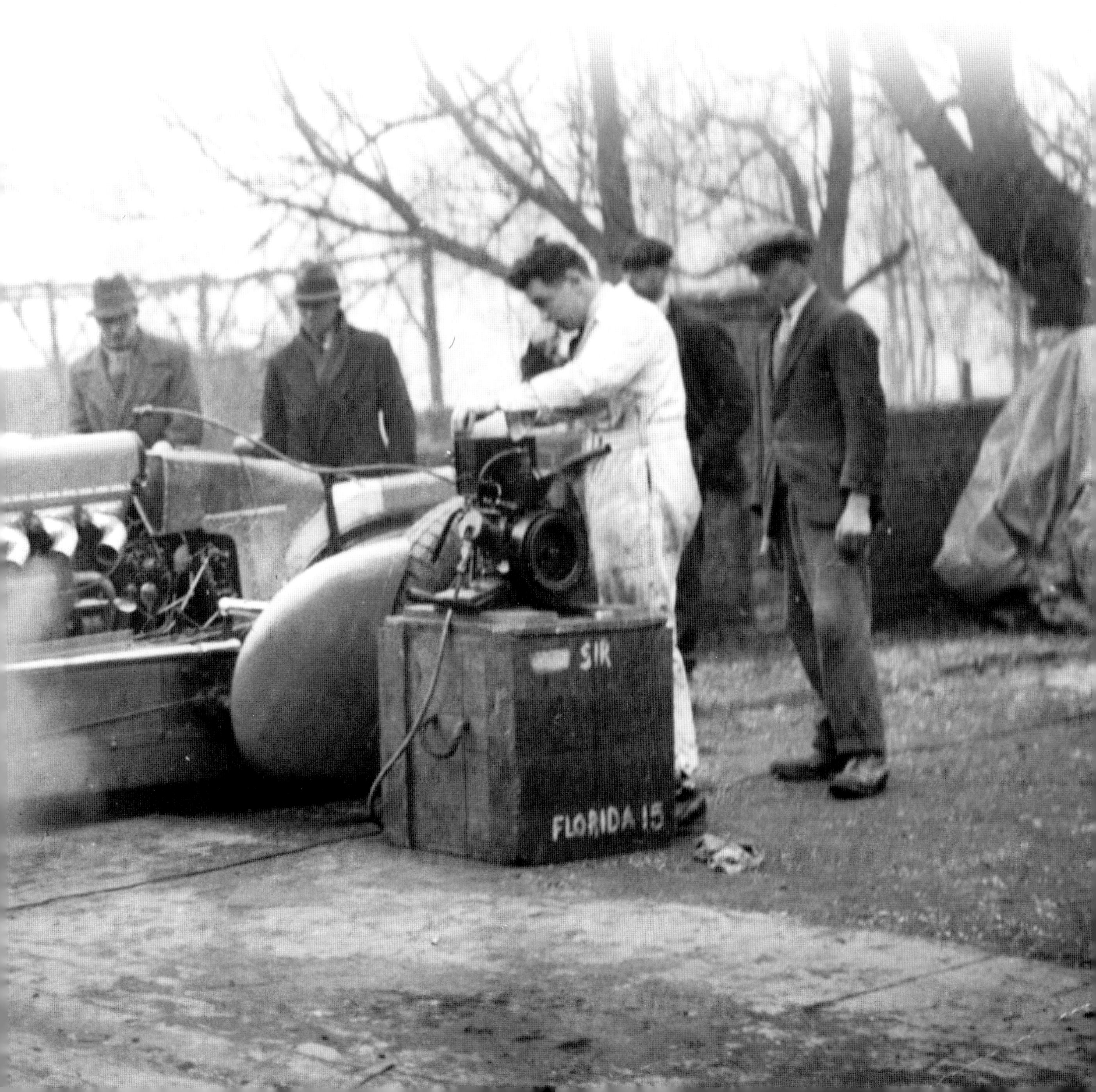
SIR
FLORIDA 15

Leo Villa OBE

As a small boy the main attraction was my father's workshop, it remained the focal point of my interest for many years to come. A vast cavernous place about 50 feet long, it housed the most powerful racing machines of their time, and I was drawn there as if by a magnet, fully immersing myself in the smell of oil, fuel, greasy tools and machinery They were wonderful things to play with if I could arrange to lay my hands on them.

Of course the workshop was Leo Villa's domain and he became my guardian angel; short, square, stubby, and in those days with tight black curly hair, his patience was as large as his smile whilst he entertained me for hours on end, providing me with the ability to handle those greasy tools with some skill whilst keeping me out of trouble.

Father's nose was apt to twitch when I meddled where I should not; his justice was swift and corporal and always most memorable. Down the years I attracted a great deal of summary punishment but with Leo's help managed to avoid many a quick tanning; I could never have done it without good old Leo.

The weekends were by far our happiest times. Father loved Sunday at home. We would see little of him during the week and on Saturday he was invariably racing at the Brooklands track or working on Blue Bird.

Sunday we often had him to ourselves and he would watch us racing around the paths in our peddle cars, one looking like a Bugatti, the other like Blue Bird. We would go out for bicycle rides, sometimes the whole family; later with Dad and Leo we would cruise the rural Surrey countryside on our motorcycles.

Pendine Sands 1927

Apparently, if he could, Father liked to have me along on these occasions and I can remember clearly playing on Pendine Sands in Wales, at the age of 6 in 1927 when he made his third attempt on the land speed record with his new custom, home-built Blue Bird. The car's initial performance was very poor after all the expense; Dad could just about slide into the cockpit behind the steering wheel, the gear box was as stiff as buggery and it was almost impossible to use and the engine kept cutting out. Every time the car stalled it jerked forward and rolled off the boards promptly sinking deep into the sand only to be dug out again immediately afterwards, to be put back on the boards.

Eventually a plough was employed to cut a furrow along the beach to drain the track; the weather got better and on 4th February the Skipper had a go and got his new world record of 174.88 mph.

Verneuk Pan 1929

Finally news came through about Verneuk Pan situated in South Africa which was described as a 'wonderful' stretch of flat land, 20 miles by 10 miles, situated 400 miles from Cape Town. Father chose this place for what was to be the biggest and most costly world record attempt yet. By the time Blue Bird was finally shipped out to South Africa her chassis and bodywork had been completely overhauled and the engine tuned to give increased power; the other alteration to the car was the position of the radiator.

For me our family trip to Verneuk Pan followed an unhappy period at Horsham and it was a welcome break to go on such a wonderful adventure in 1929 to Cape Town. Dad took the entire family with him, including our newest governess, Ivy Baker, who eventually married our butler Reg Whiteman; both remained with Jean for years. Reg looked after Dad on all his attempts and was a team member on more than one.

Jean, Donald, the Nanny and Lady Campbell.

Utah 1935

My first sight of Salt Lake City remains with me to this day. Flying through a gap in the Rocky Mountains at night, we looked downwards and ahead to see what seemed to me thousands of fairy lights of many different colours. Soon we were down and at our hotel, and I was impatient to get out to the dried-out lake, itself some 120 miles away. The next day we drove out under a blue sky and burning sun. The glare was intense yet mild compared with that at Salt Lake.

The trial runs went well and they showed that that Blue Bird would be at its limit at a shade over 300 mph. It was also clear that a major hazard would be damage to the tyres. These were specially made by Dunlops and cost around £100 each. They had fifteen layers of interwoven web canvas which were sheathed by a layer of rubber no thicker than a cigarette paper, and with no treads. This was because of the centrifugal force exerted on the tyres by high speed. Approaching 300 mph their oval shape was forced to that of a triangle. Treads would have been ripped off and Blue Bird thrown off balance.

Father was cheerful, calm, and a bit reserved when we left Wendover before the sun was up on the morning of 'the day'. I was tremendously excited but trying not to show it; it was, after all, the first time I was able to appreciate seeing him attempt a World Speed Record.

'All-ready, Sir Malcolm! Good. Let's go,' said Father. 'Best of luck, Dad.' He grinned at me, walked over to Blue Bird, clambered into the cockpit, settled himself, and adjusted his goggles. 'Right Leo!' he called and Leo started a small engine connected by hoses to Blue Bird's engine to provide her with compressed air for starting, and suddenly the beast came to life with a roar and gout of black exhaust fumes.

Leo and Donald tuck the Skipper into Blue Bird's cockpit.

With a thunderous burst and a cloud of black smoke, she was away, on track, and in a matter of moments was a small sapphire speck against the expanse of white. Suddenly she vanished. 'Quick, Leo,' I yelled. We rushed for the Lincoln, Leo at the wheel and me scrambling in beside him.

'Something's wrong,' Leo shouted. Blue Bird was out in the sun and not under the shelter having the tyres changed, but now looking as though she had been through a snowstorm; the car was surrounded by a group of mechanics, every man's face glistening with sweat. Father was standing alone a few yards away and he looked pale, grim, tired and drawn. I went over to him. 'What happened, Dad?' 'Nearside front tyre burst. I had her going at 304.'

Leo can be seen centre frame and Donald is on the other side of the car looking down at the tyre damage.

I went over to Blue Bird. The tyre was a mess; the burst of its explosion had buckled all the fairings. It was burning and giving off so much heat that it was impossible to get near it. But it was not the bursting of the tyre that was making Father look ill. During the run over the measured mile he had closed the radiator shutter to improve Blue Bird's streamlining; some aerodynamic freak occurrence had caused exhaust fumes to be sucked into the cockpit and then oil splashed all over the windscreen and Father had nearly passed out.

I stayed by Father; I had never seen him looking so grim and determined. 'Will the run back be all right, Dad?' 'Have to be boy, have to be!' Somehow I got the impression that Father felt things might go wrong again and that it might be the end. I began to worry; but there was not much I could do, and it seemed the less I said the better. Eventually Leo came over and said, 'All right now, Skipper.'

Reid Railton checks out the damage

Then with a roar Blue Bird came alive again. Another spurt of black smoke and she was off, away, and out of sight. With tensed, worried faces we clambered into the Lincoln and followed.

We saw a group round Blue Bird's canvas shelter and she was out of the sun snugly tucked away. Everything had all gone all right. 'Steady boy,' said Leo, as he pulled over towards the shelter. I was already looking for Father and opening the door. I leapt out and instantly I found myself rolling head over heels, the car had still been doing 30 mph.

Dazed, I picked myself up, stumbled along to find Father. 'Everything all right Dad?' 'Fine boy, what on earth have you done to yourself?' Blood was streaming from cuts on my face, but they didn't matter. I could have broken a leg at that moment and not noticed it. While I was being patched up, and Father was smoking and scolding me, an official rushed up to him and said, '301 miles an hour, Sir Malcolm. A new World Land Speed Record. Congratulations Sir.'

Bluebird under her shelter connected to the compressed air starter unit.

Father's face split into his cheerful grin, everybody started cheering and we hugged one another. It was a terrific moment with a mixture of emotions: exhilaration, relief after the earlier tensions, frustrations and worries and pride. Then the official returned. He looked grey, dour, worried. 'Sir Malcolm. I'm sorry. There's been a mistake.' You could feel the silence. 'Oh?' Father looked grim again. 'Yes. A check shows that the average of the two runs is 299.9 mph, not 301.'

'Bollocks,' muttered Father, then 'You're quite sure?' 'I'm afraid so!' I felt as though I had been kicked in the belly. Where there had been smiling faces all round us, now there were glum looks, querulous eyes, and frowning brows. 'I'll have another crack,' Father said. But there was nothing to be done for the time being. They knew all too well that Blue Bird had been at her peak; and the dangers of another tyre burst were playing on everybody's minds.

A little later a car pulled up and we saw the timing officials get out. They were smiling as they came towards us. 'A word with you, please, Sir Malcolm. We've re-checked the timing tapes. They confirm our first calculation. The average for the two runs was 301 mph.' Father frowned, went rather red. 'Nobody will believe it now; they will all think it is a bloody fiddle. The taste has gone.' Father grunted some more oaths… 'A fine bloody anti-climax this is.'

Lake Maggiore – Switzerland – Canton of Ticino – 1937

Dad's main preoccupation became the Blue Bird boat designed by Fred Cooper with Reid Railton, who dealt with the mechanical engineering and built by Saunders Roe. Highly advanced in design, constructed with flying-boat technology, the new Blue Bird K3 was a revolutionary single step, all wood hydroplane. It was small, lightweight and fitted with the most powerful engine available, our own Rolls-Royce R 37, turning a two-blade prop at over 10,000 revs per minute. We went up to Loch Lomond for testing in the summer of 1937.

All in all, Father was very pleased with K3's performance, but the team waited around for an entire month before the conditions of the lake were calm enough to go for the record. Those conditions never came and for the first time Dad started to endure the plague of later water speed attempts: waiting for the right conditions and accepting bad luck. However, if the surface was not smooth at speeds approaching 100 mph Blue Bird would trounce the Skipper in water, snake all over the place and bounce like a billiard ball across corrugated iron.

During the initial trials there were problems with the water-cooling system. It was complicated as the exhaust stubs were also water cooled. On one run the pressure of the water tore off the water scoop and a chunk of the transom. A new streamlined scoop was designed by Railton and built by a local Swiss engineer. Bluebird ran without its streamlined tail and cowling to help keep the engine cool. Then the cheering news came that Blue Bird had broken the World Water Speed Record, raising it to 126 mph. That was on 1st September 1937. The next day the Skipper went out again and did over 130, raising his own record to 129.5 mph.

When Dad returned home, he was not satisfied with this speed – it was too small a margin to have over Gar Wood, the previous record holder in Miss America X – and he began planning to take Blue Bird back to Switzerland the following year to the Lac Léman. He had been invited to the three-day International Speed Trials the Swiss were holding in the bay of Geneva. Again he wanted me with him and with that said I was off with Dad in pursuit of another record, this time on water.

Lac Léman - Geneva - Switzerland 1938

We drove down to Geneva in one of Dad's Bentleys, Blue Bird followed on the Adams Brothers' lorry and Leo was let loose in a Fiat with Harry and got there first. In Geneva we had exclusive use of a slip outside the main town in Corsier and a local firm laid on an electric hoist to launch the Bird, the Société Nautique de Genève provided hangar space for the hydroplane, equipment, spare engine and aviation fuel.

The whole outing was a grand, exciting holiday for me; I was now a big boy and Leo no longer had to keep me occupied by finding split pins but was able to give me odd jobs to do when the engine was being worked on. We were out on the lake every morning at 3 a.m. and I listened to the long discussions Leo had with Father about Blue Bird and getting all the possible speed out of her. There were as always various complications and she was not moving as quickly as he hoped. With the team was Sid Randal, chief engineer from Adams Bros, the transport company responsible for moving Blue Bird from England. Sid was a first-class mechanic and accompanied Father on all his speed boat record attempts.

Speed trials held in the bay of Geneva, 1938.

Lake Hallwil - Switzerland 1938

The record attempt was not going well on the Lac Léman; Blue Bird would not do more than 126 mph, so Albert Schmidt, the President of the Geneva Yacht Club, told Dad that he knew a lake close to the Swiss German border called Hallwilersee which would be more suitable as it was much smaller (8.5 km x 1.5 km), well sheltered and without any pleasure craft. A boathouse and slip were built for Blue Bird and the attempt was on. We moved over to Hallwil and from September our base was the Brestenburg Hotel at the head of the lake whose shores were shrouded in trees and dotted with castles. The water was flat calm and conditions were good; Blue Bird was running at her absolute peak on a knife's edge, but still inclined to be very unstable.

During trials she roared, belched thick black smoke and shot out vast plumes of white spray behind her, the sound of the Rolls engine echoing around the mountains. On 16th September, Father increased his world record slightly to 130.9 mph, but neither Leo nor I saw Blue Bird racing over the measured mile for we were in a boat moored at the beginning of the run-up. We watched Father streak off, listened to the boat's distant thunder and then saw him coasting back to us. He was pleased with the result but determined to go even faster.

Joe Adams, Albert Schmidt, Harry Leach, Malcolm, Reid Railton, Leo and Sid Randall.

Albert Schmidt with the timing team from Longines in St Imier.

Coniston Water 1939

The new Bluebird K4 arrived in her temporary boathouse at Coniston on the afternoon of 13th August 1939; the weather was stunning, the lake like a mill pond.

Bluebird, brand new, looking sleek and powerful in her coat of deep sapphire, was lying on a cradle in a temporary boathouse on a slipway beside Pier House from which steamers plied up and down the lake. The cradle was on rails running into the lake. We looked her over, and then went to our hotel, impatient for the morrow. Leo rehearsed me for the christening ceremony and, with my mind more on seeing her in action on the lake, and with Father smiling and a big crowd round, I declared, 'I name this craft Blue Bird. May God bless her, her pilot and all who work with her.' A bottle of Mercier Champagne cracked and fizzed and a stream of effervescent bubbles slid and dripped; Bluebird moved slowly down the slip into the lake stern first and then Father went out to her in a small launch, settled himself in the cockpit and, with a burst of flame from her exhausts, K4 shot away in a cloud of spray for her first run.

The Slipper - Coniston 1947

After just a few trial runs the Skipper set a new water speed record of 141.74 mph, a clear 16.98 mph above Gar Wood's last average. By 8.30 a.m. we were all at breakfast, with congratulations rolling in for Father and his new record. The sun was still shining and everything had gone off with a sweet reasonableness not always associated with records. Father was elated that the entire attempt had taken just six days.

Following the interlude of the second World War Father turned turned his attention back to the water speed record he still held. The war had forced the development of more efficient types of propulsion and the next logical step was to build a jet-powered Blue Bird to exceed 200 mph that would see the record out of reach of any future American competitor for many years to come.

So, aged 63 with failing health and badly degenerating eyesight, Father had K4 modified by Vospers and a Goblin II jet engine was installed. During trials, again on Coniston the boat proved to be completely unstable and uncontrollable when approaching 90 mph in her new form. Modifications at Vospers were carried out under the supervision of Peter Du Cane, followed by trials in Poole harbour with reasonable success. Back up on Coniston for speed trials, the K4 Slipper, as she was known, now started porpoising at speeds over 100 mph with such violence that Father was almost ejected out of the cockpit.

About the same time I became interested in the development of a portable power-driven bench-saw and, upon meeting two brothers named Meldrum, who were producing movie projector spares and equipment, agreed to join forces with them to bring out a completely new line of woodworking machine tools. I put my small amount of capital earned during the war into their company, Kiné Engineering Co. Ltd, at Horley, and settled down to business life, eventually becoming chairman. It was also at this time that Lewis Norris, who had trained as a marine engineer and had just returned from Burma working with the Burma Oil Company, joined Kiné as workshop manager; soon after he was followed by his brother Eric, who became our accountant.

Life had not gone well for Dad since the war. The new jet-driven Blue Bird was a brute of a thing and thoroughly unstable, and Dad's eyes were giving him terrible trouble and he was now in St Mary's Hospital, Paddington, where he had undergone an operation; he was feeling under the weather when I arrived, which distressed me considerably, and both of us had tears in our eyes when I left his room.

By November Father was seriously ill, and I insisted on sending for a specialist. He came to Little Gatton and that night we learned that Father could never recover: it was only a matter of time before the end, which began on 23rd December. I was sitting in my office at Horley when Father's housekeeper rang. 'Your Father has had a stroke. Can you come immediately?' I tore up the road to Reigate; Little Gatton was empty, save for Father who was in a darkened bedroom. I saw him lying, haggard, scarcely able to move or to speak above a whisper. The stroke had paralysed the whole of his left side. I kneeled at his bedside and broke down. Father, with an effort, pulled out the handkerchief in my jacket pocket. He dried my eyes and said, 'It's all right, old chap, I'm quite finished.'

Jean and I nursed him that night, and Father hung on grimly. He had been looking forward to Christmas and a family reunion, but we decided not to tell him when it was Christmas Day. Unfortunately he found out from the nurse. 'I do hate being taken for a bloody fool,' he whispered. 'Why didn't you tell me?' Then he added, 'Go and get a bottle of champagne, boy.' I returned shortly, and, despite his failing strength and partial paralysis, Father had everybody brought to his room. The bottle was opened, our glasses filled. Father asked to be raised up. With a glass in his right hand he whispered, 'A Merry Christmas to everybody.' A few hours later he fell unconscious. He died at 3 minutes to midnight on 31st December 1948. We laid him to rest at Chislehurst in the same plot as his parents.

Reigate, Surrey - January 1949

We sipped whisky, the last bottle at Little Gatton, and let our thoughts roam back to the past events of the weeks since Father died. I was sitting at his desk in his book-lined study with an old family friend, Goldie Gardner, another racing driver and record breaker, who had come regularly to Little Gatton to visit Father before his passing.

We talked of the funeral at Chislehurst, and the memorial service at St Margaret's, where there had not been an empty pew. We talked of tomorrow's public auction of the contents of the house for the final stage in the winding up of Father's estate. Everything we had known as children was to be put up for sale; we were allowed to buy before the auction anything with sentimental attachment. I bought the old 1935 Bluebird car and the Bluebird K4 hydroplane with so many happy memories for me of Coniston in 1939. I stared morosely at Reigate through the study windows and sipped my whisky. Goldie reminisced nostalgically about Father, his determination and dislike of being beaten at anything on which he had set his mind.

Then he asked me if I had heard that the multi-millionaire American industrialist, Henry Kaiser, had announced that he was going to take the World Water Speed Record back to America and that he had commissioned an all-aluminium speedboat, costing in the region of $150,000. Guy Lombardo, the band leader, was running it on the Potomac River and was after the Old Man's record! We talked on for a while and then Goldie left.

Goldie and Malcolm, Daytona Beach, Florida, 1935

ALTAR OF SPEED
1949–1955

I had got the bug. It broke up my marriage. My wife could not understand my dedication... my second marriage was also sacrificed on the altar of speed; it was the only thing that mattered to me...

Donald Campbell CBE

He's going to take the water speed record back to the States. The words bounced around inside my head like a ping-pong ball, as I continued to chain smoke and sip whisky. I wondered what Dad's reaction would be if I told him I was thinking of having a go! I had a flash of his nose twitching with annoyance and a stream of images: Brooklands, South Africa, Utah 1935, Geneva and Hallwil, Coniston in 1939 with the beautiful sapphire and silver Bluebird* streaking down the lake, and dear old Dad's jubilant smiles when he learnt he had increased his own water speed record. His last.

Suddenly the anger overwhelmed me and I said out loud... 'Bugger you Kaiser! I'll have a bloody crack at it myself. We'll give you a run for your money!' I paced round the study agitated, reflecting upon my decision, confused and excited. I had never even been in a racing boat or a racing car for that matter; I started to focus and wonder how long it would be before we could get Bluebird back up to Coniston and on the water again.

In a cloud of adrenaline and whisky vapour I dug out old Leo from the workshop where he was clearing up after the misery left after anyone's passing. Except that he had lost his curly black hair, looked older with more lines on his face, now 49 and wiser, but he was always the same old cheerful Leo, thorough and dependable, my oldest friend from the days at Povey when he had kept me out of so much trouble.

*Note: Donald Campbell took over record breaking from Sir Malcolm in 1949 and changed the spelling of The Blue Bird to Bluebird.

Guy Lombardo, who raced speed boats by day and conducted his orchestra by night.

I blurted: 'Leo! Kaiser is going to try to take Dad's water speed record back to America and I'm going to do something about it! *Are you with me?*' He looked me very steadily in the eye and said, 'Before you start this thing Don, I'll tell you but two things: once you start you'll never be able to stop and no matter how long you are at it, you will never, ever, get used to the atmosphere.' On both counts he was absolutely *right*!

He slapped me on the back and we both burst out laughing, but Leo was the only one preoccupied with my decision; my wife Daphne just took it in her stride, looking at it like as a fairly harmless pastime, a way to keep me out of mischief whilst she was looking after our 12-month-old daughter Georgina.

For me the intention was a short once-in-a-lifetime bash at it. Certainly I never saw it as a threat to my marriage or as a life changer. Perhaps Leo was right and I was just a little too young and innocent to really understand what I was getting myself into. But by August I would be back up at Coniston with Dad's old team and Bluebird K4 converted back to propeller drive. The first shock I got as a would-be record breaker was the sheer amount of work involved in organising the project.

So for six months we worked frantically on the boat and during this period I became more involved and acquainted with Lew Norris who had been working with me at Kiné. Lew worked for a while with Reid Railton on Bluebird K4 making improvements with my very limited budget, and progressively at this time I found myself telling Daphne, 'Sorry not now darling; no not tomorrow. Can't it wait until after the record?'

Leo and I paid a visit to Coniston to make arrangements for launching, slipping and housing the boat. I was happy, though a little nostalgic, to be back at Coniston, and to meet once more Connie Robinson and her husband, who ran the Bull Hotel, and could never do too much to help us; and also Goffy Thwaites, the grand old Coniston boatman. We found, for various reasons, that we could use only part of the slipway from 1939 next to Pier Cottage, and we decided to house the boat under temporary steel scaffolding and tarpaulins.

Godfrey 'Goffy' Thwaites, Coniston Boatman.

In a flash the port plane dipped violently, Bluebird swerved round, snaked and headed towards a boat of photographers narrowly missing them by 10 feet but covering their boat heavily in spray. How Bluebird did not turn turtle was beyond me. I took a deep breath, held the wheel, composed myself whilst still travelling at over 100 and straightened her up on track down the centre of the course. I had had my first taste of cold fear. 'Take it easy you bloody fool', I thought. 'Good old Leo; he knows exactly what he is talking about. Listen to him boy.' And there he was waiting for me at the end of the course. 'Well ... Speed King?' he questioned innocently as I stepped out of the cockpit. I looked at him straight in the eye and with a half-smile. 'Leo this job's fucking dangerous!' Everybody in the launch roared with laughter. I had just learnt my first lesson as a record breaker. Unc assured me that there were plenty more to come.

We got busy again with Bluebird and decided to go for the record three days later, and reserved the timekeepers and officials. Then, as always, the weather changed and held us up until the following week. During this period the realisation of what I had got myself into came to full light and that record-breaking is not just an adventure but can be a very grim affair. Of course I was frightened, but fear is a very private thing which I could not share with Leo or Daphne. She had enough to worry about already. As I climbed into that cockpit at dawn I would have given everything to be a million miles away from Coniston. It was unearthly quiet and the lake was an eerie place, misty and uninviting. Once Leo had left in the support boat I had never felt so alone in all my life, floating there in the middle of the lake with the water gently lapping against the sides of the Bird.

With Jean on the pier by Pier Cottage.

This time I was tense. I knew exactly what I was about to face as I accelerated Bluebird up to 150; by the time I passed the marker boys at the start of the measured mile my foot was hard down. Suddenly halfway through the mile there was a puff of smoke and scalding black oil sprayed across the windscreen and caught part of my face. Instinctively my foot came off the throttle and at that speed it was the worst thing to do: as the power came off, Bluebird went for a crazy sideways skid of some 200 yards in under a second. I had no more control of her than a runaway rocket. I hit the throttle hard again and turned the helm right over as far it would go and got her back on track. As death receded my fears returned.

The second run was uneventful except for Bluebird's sluggishness. I put my foot right down again but she did not respond with anywhere near the same vigour, still, I hoped that there was a chance we had just clipped the old record. Then over the radio link to the launch at the start of the mile the great news came: 'You've done it!' Proud and relieved that the whole ordeal was over, Daphne was standing next to Leo as I came ashore. I had not realised until then that this private adventure of mine had not been much fun for her. 'It's all over now, we'll soon be home darling, and my God it will be good to be there.'

I heard the record announced on the BBC eight o'clock news. It was now public: Campbell again! I just finished talking to Leo when suddenly the timekeepers turned up at the Black Bull Hotel looking a little sheepish. I thought to myself, I've seen that look before; Utah 1935. 'I'm terribly sorry Donald but we made a mistake, in fact you were two miles an hour under your father's record.' To be quite honest I was not at all surprised; it was clear to me from the beginning that there was no way breaking this record was going to be that easy. However the news was shattering. Later, whilst checking Bluebird Leo found that the oil had come from the gearbox which had collapsed, and the return run had severely damaged the prop shaft and bearings. We spent a gloomy couple of days packing up. There is a spot where the road bends where you get a last view of Coniston stretched out amidst the hills and in the morning I drove off with Daphne. I stopped the car and got out. It was almost ten years to the day that I had stood there with Dad, but he had got his record, I had not. I could see him standing there next to me as clear as a bell. As I gazed back at Coniston I muttered to myself: 'Bitch! We'll be back next year!'

46

Far left: Goffie Thwaites, the Adam Brothers, Daphne in the cockpit, Donald, Sid Randall, Leo, Harry Leach, Tim Villa (Leo's son).

Relationships

With Dorothy in the South of France.

Donald and Daphne Campbell.

One of the ways in which I did react strongly against my father was over my first marriage. I have always liked women and so did he: he was very handsome and enjoyed an enormous amount of success with the ladies. But for him, family life was a very stormy affair. None of his three marriages was a success and he was never, ever, prepared to make any compromise whatsoever over his record-breaking activities in the interest of a marriage. You have to put your family considerations to one side, you've got to be selfish in this line of work, and I have inherited this attitude from him. Lady Dorothy, my own mother, never learnt how to handle Malcolm; rightly she could not accept his infidelities and understand his many motivations, nor did any other woman for that matter. In turn, this made him react violently when I told him in 1945 that I was in love and was going to marry Daphne Harvey. 'Well my boy, you're 24 and that is old enough to make a bloody fool out of yourself: I can't stop you and I won't ... don't expect any money ... don't expect me at the wedding!'

The dilemma of my first two marriages was not so much any basic incompatibly: Dorothy and Daphne were admirable wives and I was very fond of them, but it was simply that my life as a record breaker got far too much for them to handle. They failed to keep up with my level of intoxication, but then if record-breaking really is an addiction, as Leo predicted, how did I succumb to it in the first place? I feel now that it was not so much my boyhood, nor my relations with Father. I was sure now that, for me, it had begun with my failure to win the World Water Speed Record with Bluebird K4 on Coniston. That's what triggered it.

I was convinced that if I had succeeded then I may have escaped and there is a very good chance that I may have settled firmly into a routine of a respectable and reasonably successful business life. As far as my own success concerns me, if I had taken the record in 1949 I would probably have written the whole endeavour off as a short, agreeable episode in the rich tapestry of life and that would almost certainly have been that. This was what Daphne was hoping for, but I failed, and failure is one thing us Campbells don't handle well. Goldie Gardner once told me that Dad was a world beater only because of all the setbacks he had in the very beginning at Saltburn in 1922 and Fanöe in Denmark in 1923. Each time he got the land speed record he failed to have it recognised officially because of disagreements over the legitimacy of the timing apparatus. It made him so furious that after that there was no holding him back.

I have only known one woman who has been able to cope with my obsession with record-breaking and that is my third wife, Ms Tonia Bern. As a glamorous and international cabaret entertainer she has a successful professional career of her own and that certainly helps a woman who wants to stay married to anyone in my line of business. She has always been realistic about this passion of mine and has never tried to fight it. 'So long as you're not jealous of my singing,' she says, 'I'll promise not to be jealous of your record-breaking.' She told me soon after we met, 'let's face it darling. You're just not the sort of guy who enjoys keeping regular hours and likes coming home to his slippers. And you are certainly not the kind of guy a girl can lean on.' For Tonia this is all right; for my first two wives it was all wrong.

Tonia Bern-Campbell and Donald, 1966.

Gina

Living and growing up with a father called Donald Campbell had wonderful moments, but for a man of his calibre and driven to the extent he was to attain speed record after speed record had some difficulties. For an only child the biggest downside was the amount of time he wasn't around, wasn't at home, and he never came to school sports days, never had the time to show much interest in what was going on in my young life. Strangely I didn't feel it at the time, because what you've never had you never miss; it's on reflection that I'm more aware of what was missing, just a bit.

The upsides, though, were just amazing and the entrée into another world of celebrities and visiting places that a young child would never have had access to in that era were really mind blowing: travelling across the world, seeing and meeting so many influential people from many walks of life. A glance through our visitor's book bears testament to this. Funnily enough though, I didn't realise my Dad was 'famous' as he had always been famous, so it was just the norm to me then. Now I realise what an incredible person, man, father and national/international superstar he was. Home life yo-yoed from mother to stepmother to stepmother and various most attractive 'Social Secretaries,' Dad's eupherism for his lady friends in-between ... life was never dull, that was for sure, and, luckily for my self-preservation, I was very adaptable and probably learnt how to deal with these big changes in personnel that came through our home. But life is for learning and changing ... nothing is forever!

Gina Campbell, 2016

They Rode Together

During the winter of 1950 the battered old Bluebird was back in our workshop in the stable of the Reigate Hill Hotel. Why I needed this challenge of setbacks to get me going I could not understand. All I know is that during that very long winter all I desired was that record, and with an intensity that I had never felt for anything in my life before. It had become an obsession. My mornings would be filled with arranging the scores of administrative details connected with the record bid; when they were finished I had my work at Kiné to take care of. That would keep me busy until seven or eight and after that I would ultimately be with Leo and his son Tim in the workshop working on the boat.

Daphne was with Gina and it was about this time that my first marriage started to go to pieces, and Daphne decided to take Gina to go and stay with Mother. I was told that I had changed and that she wanted a man she could depend on, and she was tired of being married to a bloke having an affair with an old boat. This was quite true, but I was past the point of no return and I could not do much about it as I existed for one thing only now. I went to stay with my sister Jean and her husband in Surrey, and decided that henceforth it was a bachelor's life for me and it was obviously unfair to expect any woman to put up with the sort of thing Daphne had to.

It was all I needed as a spur to success; I was certainly to have enough of it during the summer of 1950. We had been experimenting during that winter with a model of Bluebird K4 at the Admiralty Experimental Works near Gosport. These trials in the water tank and the wind tunnel showed that the boat's maximum speed was between 150 and 155 mph. My father's record of 141 mph still stood, and in the hope of squeezing just a few more miles an hour out of Bluebird we had had a new propeller designed for her. We left for Coniston at the end of June with high hopes of achievement. But from the start there were delays, the weather was bad and the propeller took longer to arrive from the manufacturers than we expected.

'I want to ride with you in the boat', Leo stated. 'If we are going to have any trouble with the nose rising at high speed then two pairs of eyes are better than one.' Frankly I was not keen on this idea at all and really did not want Leo to share the risks; but he was quite adamant and, admiring his courage, we fitted a second cockpit next to me in the boat so he could ride alongside to observe the instruments and monitor the behaviour and trim of the craft. It was while we were involved in this work that Leo heard a news bulletin over the radio.

He came running down to the edge of the water, waving his arms frantically to attract our attention shouting out that he had bad news: an American named Stanley Sayers had pushed the water speed record up to over 160. Nobody knew who in the hell Sayers was, we had never even heard of him, all we knew was that he called his boat Slo-Mo-Shun. Gradually more news filtered through to us: she had won all the major racing events in America that year and it was soon clear that Sayers was using a new principle to reach those sorts of speeds. But no one seemed to know more than that. It was eventually Lew Norris and Reid Railton that explained this new performance and as they connected the behaviour of Slo-Mo-Shun with what had happened to Bluebird when I blew up the engine.

Slo-Mo-Shun IV, Lake Washington. Stanley Sayers was a successful 53-year-old unlimited powerboat racer and the president of the American Automobile Company. He is seen here with Ted Jones, his riding mechanic, and the hydroplane's designer, an engineer at the Boeings aircraft factory and a powerboat racer in his own right. The all-wood three-point hydroplane was powered by a 2,000 hp Allison Aero engine through a step-up 3:1 water-cooled gearbox, spinning the prop at 12,000 revolutions per minute.

Oltranza Cup - Lake Garda, Italy

It was obvious now that the Rolls-Royce engine had blown up because the stern of the boat rose so high out of the water that the scoop taking in the cooling water was no longer submerged and the engine, starved, had overheated. Bluebird had started to ride on three points: the planing shoes under the front floats and the propeller's boss at the stern. This was prop-riding. It was the reduction in drag from the stern lifting up out of the water that gave the extra speed. This was a start; we carried on our research and finally found that at really high speeds not just the stern but the propeller shaft, part of the rudder and one of the propeller blades came out of the water as well. The reduction in drag was terrific and from everything we could discover Slo-Mo-Shun worked on exactly this principle.

Lew and Reid redesigned Bluebird and all the winter of 1950 we worked feverishly in the barn to convert her into a prop-rider. It was a complicated job: we had to move the engine forward 6 feet to change the centre of gravity enabling the stern to come up, and we had to make changes to the floats, planing shoes and the cockpit arrangements. Finally we had her finished by the spring of 1951 and following an invitation, I decided that we would try out the boat properly for the first time in a racing circuit competition on Lake Garda in Italy for the Oltranza Cup. This was a closed circuit race for some of the fastest speedboats in the world, and it had never, ever, been won by Great Britain. When the converted prop-riding Bluebird won the trophy and set a new lap record of 159 km/h (100 mph) we all felt we were finally getting somewhere near Slo-Mo-Shun's performance.

Late that autumn we were back up at Coniston with a lot of work to finish on Bluebird. A high speed boat is a very delicate and highly strung creature and at one point this one was making spectacular corkscrew leaps on each run. It was only on 24th October that we had her balanced and trimmed for high speed. Leo was in his cockpit alongside me on the fastest run we ever made in that boat. At last we had everything as it should be, and on that October morning I knew for the first time that we could definitely get the record back from Sayers. It was a great moment as I saw the needle on the air speed indicator sweep smoothly up to 150 mph and then on to 160 mph; 170 mph. I glanced briefly at Leo, and said to myself, 'my God boy this is way past the record, we got it!'

This was too good to be true and it was at the very moment that the thought crossed my mind and Bluebird was just coming out of the measured mile when there was an enormous crash that was heard 7 miles away and the boat went mad, the vibration became intense and she skidded across the lake, left and right, as I cut the power. Simultaneously Leo cut the fuel and, in silence, we drifted to a stop. It was all over so swiftly that there was no time for fear. We just floated there dazed for a few minutes trying to understand what had happened.

One of the launches was nearby, and we got a line aboard and towed frantically for the shore. But Bluebird's decks were awash in a matter of minutes and finally we swam for it in the freezing cold water. One of the launches picked us up and I then watched as all our hopes for the World Water Speed Record slipped slowly beneath the waves of Coniston, about 20 yards from the shore. We got her up the next morning; at first it seemed like we had hit a railway sleeper: there was a huge hole in the hull and the machinery was so much mangled metal. Leo and I looked at the wreck of all we had worked on for the last three years. Lewis told us that it was the bracket that was supporting the prop shaft that had given way under the enormous pressure. The prop shaft had whipped, made its way through the hull and pulled the gearbox out of its mountings, which explained the big hole running the length of Bluebird.

K4 went to Bill Coley's yard in Hounslow and what was left of the mangled machinery was scrapped. There seemed no point in going on, then the news came again that Stanley Sayers had increased his own mark to 178 mph and we knew by then that Reid was working with John Cobb on a jet-propelled, reverse three-point hydroplane called Crusader. The record had gone into a class in which it seemed for the moment I had no hope of competing. No more for you old lad, I told myself. From now on it's regular hours and a bowler hat for you matey. Kiné was doing very well and there was more than enough work to keep me busy. I had bought myself Abbotts, a 500-year-old cottage just outside Dorking and actually did feel that the time may have come to settle down at last.

Little Abbotts, Betchworth, Surrey

In 1952 I married for the second time. Dorothy McKegg, my new wife, was a New Zealander. She was a music student in London and we had first met up at Coniston when she had been touring the Lakes with a friend. Most of our courting had been done against a backdrop of record bids, mechanical problems and trial runs. I suppose, at least Dorothy must have had a clearer idea of what she was in for when she married me than Daphne. All the same, I noticed that Dorothy, like Daphne before her, seemed delighted with the idea that I may be settling down at last. Perhaps this marriage had a better hope of succeeding now that Bluebird was on the scrapheap. Unfortunately for our future together, a catastrophe was to occur which brought about a new career and a period of family neglect.

On 29th September Crusader had crashed at about 220 mph on Loch Ness and John Cobb had been killed. I decided there and then when I heard the news that the time really had come for me to carry on with the pursuit of higher speeds on water and to start where John had left off. I had known him since my boyhood at Brooklands. I liked the man very much and admired him greatly; he was a bold visionary as well as a very, very, brave man. His death was perhaps inevitable, for he was the first pilot to enter a new phase in the pursuit of the water speed record. The barrier was unforgiving and so was the surface of the water if it was not perfect: flat like a mill pond, almost impossible conditions when you are ready to run, but easy to observe when you are idle because of the technicalities of the programme.

There was a lot of talk about a mysterious water barrier, like the sound barrier in the air. It had destroyed Crusader and all the armchair critics said it would smash any other boat that tried to penetrate the realms of 200 mph on water. Personally I was totally unconvinced that this water barrier even existed and that there was any sort impenetrable wall holding back the speed of water-borne craft any more than there was for land or air-bound craft.

Lew Norris and his brother Ken were as fascinated as I was in the technical problem of high speed on water. With Ken and Lew I talked over the Cobb disaster and we decided that we would benefit and learn from Vospers' mistakes. Then we would build a boat so revolutionary that it would break the water barrier and go far beyond the realms of any other before.

It took us nearly three years to design and build the Bluebird K7 jet-hydroplane and we began by studying every inch of 16 mm film we could find of the last few vital seconds of Crusader's last run. All the spare funds I had went into the design work and eventually ran out.

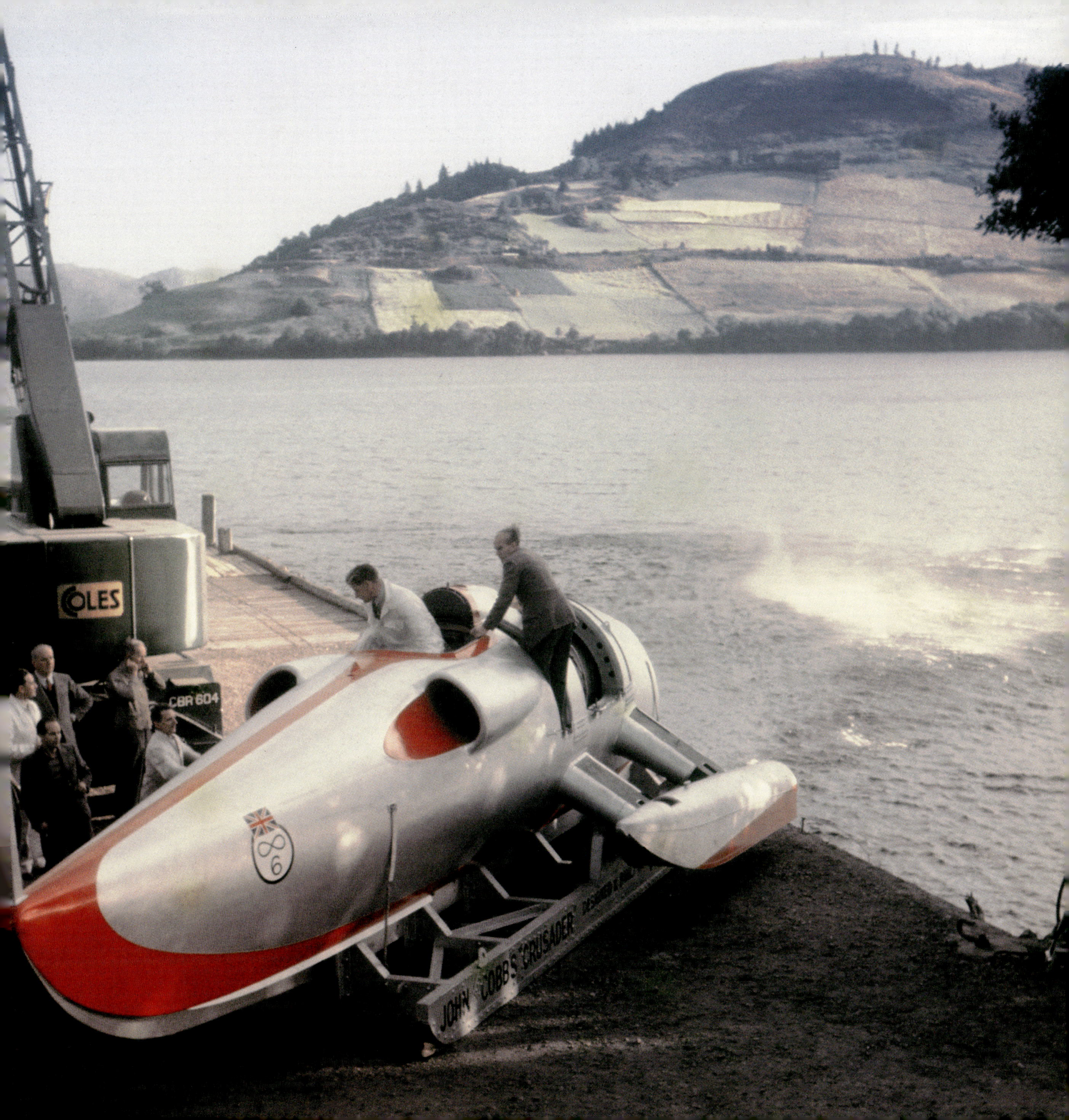
COLES
CBR 604
6
JOHN COBB'S "CRUSADER"

Crusader

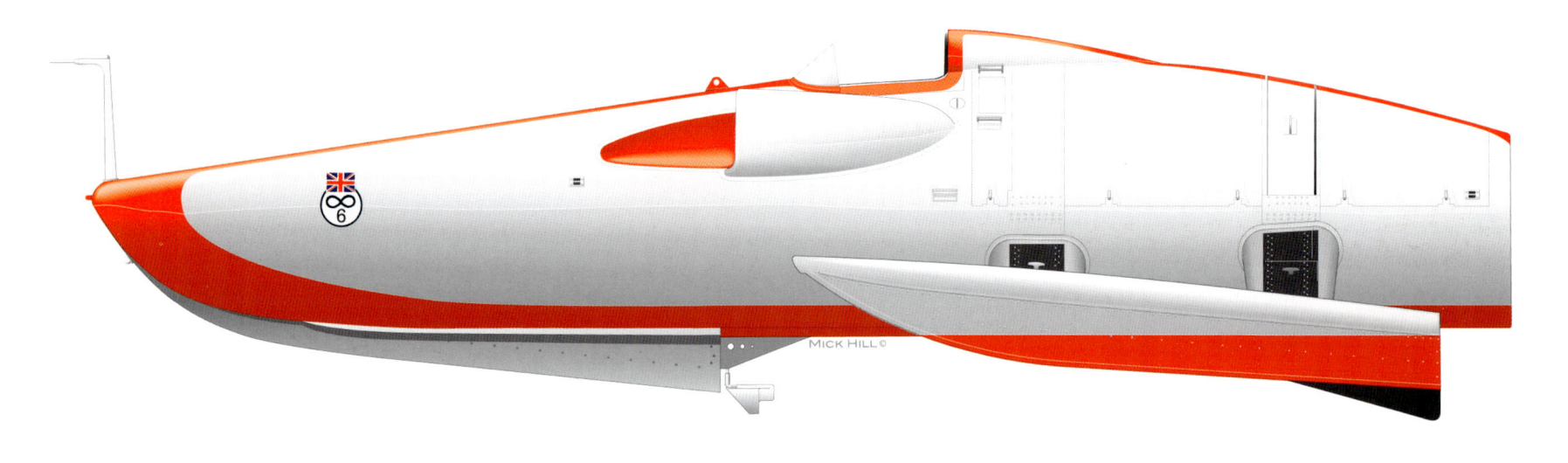

Reid Railton was a design genius, a master of engineering packaging that took ideas from many disciplines and included them into his design concepts, while always being more than a step ahead of the opposition. When Cobb decided he would take on the World Water Speed Record, Railton was the only man for the job. There was no one else in the world qualified to take on the task, especially as the speed sought was far above any considered before.

The choice of Vospers as builder was a simple one. They had turned Railton's ideas for Blue Bird K4 into a record breaker, and though Railton had looked at aircraft manufacturers for the construction of Crusader, he and Cobb decided that their limited knowledge of boat construction outweighed their own knowledge of high speed. Railton furnished Vospers with a rough outline, and several concept drawings for what was to become Crusader, and documentation between the parties clearly shows that Railton's advanced ideas didn't sit well with Vospers' traditional methods and thinking. The design concept was Railton's and what Vospers agreed to do was to turn Railton's thought's and detailed sketches, into a set of drawings, from which their in-house build team could construct what was to be the world's fastest boat. It was then that trouble began.

The design was a leap into the unknown and it is odd to see Railton calculating towards the upper limits of what was possible, taking into account the materials available at the time, and Vospers' conservative thinking. Vospers were experienced in 'high speed' craft: motor torpedo and rescue crafts. Railton had a firm grasp on how the faster one went, the harder things became. If one subject sums up the conflict between designer and builder, it is the very part that the whole project rested on, literally: the planing surfaces.

Crusader was a three-point hydroplane; at speed the craft would be supported by three 'points'. This reduced hydrodynamic drag, and increased speed. The faster you travel on water, the harder the medium becomes. What at low speed allows you to glide through becomes like concrete.

Railton calculated the likely loads the planing shoes were to encounter and these figures were in the tonnes. To counteract them he envisaged three metal rings within the hull, the rear most supporting the engine and the rear of the rear planeing sponsons. Further forward, another ring held the front of the engine and the front of the rear sponsons. And further forward another ring would hold the rudder mechanism and support the rear of the forward planeing shoe, the one that would hit the water first, and hardest. These rings would be taking the crafts' weight, and dissipate the loads as Crusader rode on the water in excess of 200 mph. To ensure this meeting between the fast and the immovable object, was as smooth as possible, Railton had drawn a 'V' profile on the bottom of the planing shoes, to separate the water to either side.

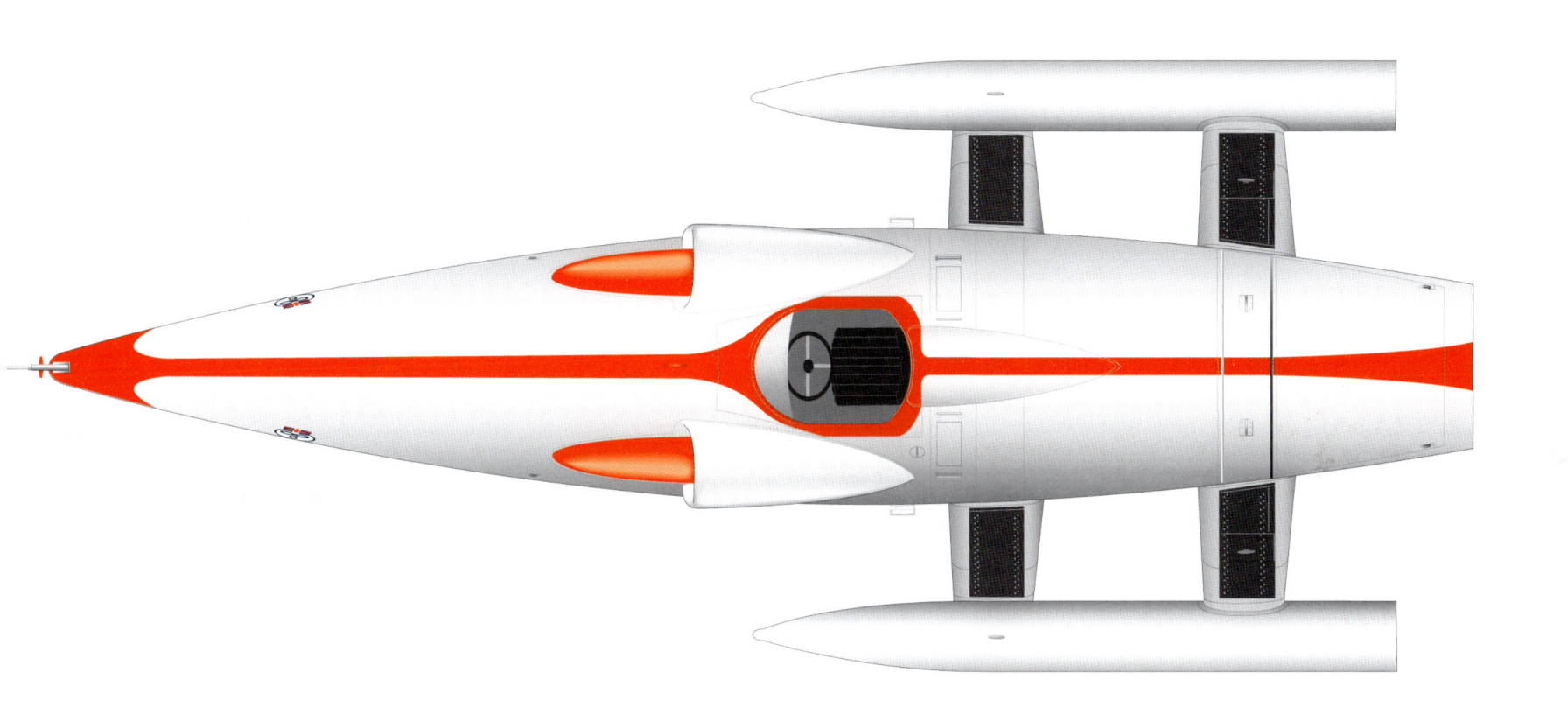

Over the months that followed, Railton was slowly overruled, until eventually, only the metal hoops for the engine were included. Peter Du Cane of Vospers actually stated in print that Railton had 'over calculated' the likely impact loads, as well as the effects a large, unbraced rudder would have on the hull. Sadly, as the attempt wore on, it became apparent that the effects were considerable, as the forward shoe was 'strengthened' on a daily basis, until Du Cane asked that the vessel be taken back to Vospers to have the work done, 'properly'. This all placed Cobb in a intractable situation, and when finally the weather looked well set for an all out attempt, it is said he promised he would only just exceed the record, and then allow Vospers time to rectify what Du Cane described as a design problem.

Sadly, it is here that the efficiency of Railton's concept backfired, as what would be perfect for going as fast as possible became the last nail in a failure. The faster a boat travels, the more the drag of the water increases, the speed/drag curve. The design of Crusader was such, that at high speed, the speed/drag curve became a flat line, and even with a closed throttle, the boat would continue at speed, if not actually continue to accelerate. Also, and untested by Cobb himself (though it was by Du Cane at low speed), a larger, fabricated rudder had been fitted in lieu of the small, knife-edge, cast rudder.

As with all accidents, all these components now became one in disaster and John Cobb crashed to his death.

Ignoring the analysis of the time, the accident has been subject to a newer investigation, with the aid of modern technology, and it becomes more likely that the slow collapse of the front shoe, linked to an increase in rudder 'flutter', created by the rudder slowly becoming more exposed to high-speed water as the shoe collapsed, caused the rudder to tear off its mount, and up into the hull, creating a scoop causing the largely unsupported rear end of the forward shoe to collapse up as well, filling the hull with water and bursting it apart from the inside. Indeed, slow-motion-enhanced footage of the accident shows a plume of water escaping the cockpit before the final dive into the lake.

Modern-day calculations confirm that Railton's figures for the impact loads were actually quite conservative, and these were over five times what Vospers considered likely.

Steve Holter, Belves, France, 2016

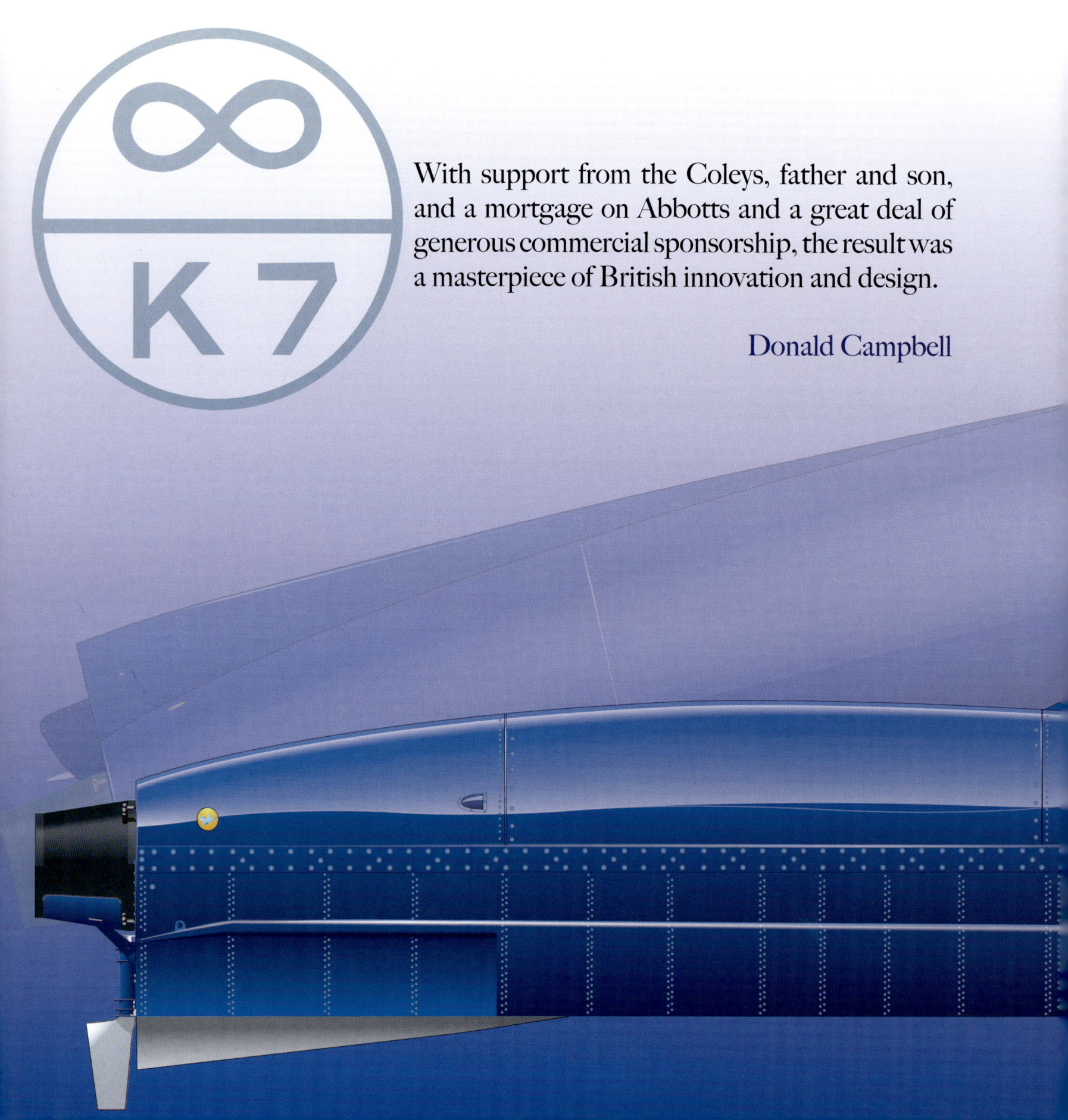

> With support from the Coleys, father and son, and a mortgage on Abbotts and a great deal of generous commercial sponsorship, the result was a masterpiece of British innovation and design.
>
> Donald Campbell

Campbell-Norris Bluebird hydroplane in her 1955 Ullswater configuration.

Norris Brothers Ltd,
Burgess Hill, Sussex, England

Lew Norris had designed the new running gear mounts for K4 and in 1951 he had undertaken initially, aided by Reid Railton, the design work for the boat's conversion to prop-rider. By 1952 Norris Brothers Ltd, consultant engineers, was established and the partners were Lewis Norris, his brother Eric, Kine's accountant, and the younger Ken who had been involved with another water speed record attempt using a jet-powered hydrofoil. Donald was later elected chairman.

Walter, Leslie, Kenneth, Lewis and Eric.

The 'C' Boat is born

Such was Donald's desire to go on with the pursuit of higher speeds on water that the Coley family offered financial backing towards the construction of a new prop-rider to go for the Harmsworth Trophy. Lew and Ken prepared some general arrangement drawings for a screw-powered racing craft to bring the coveted trophy back to England from America.

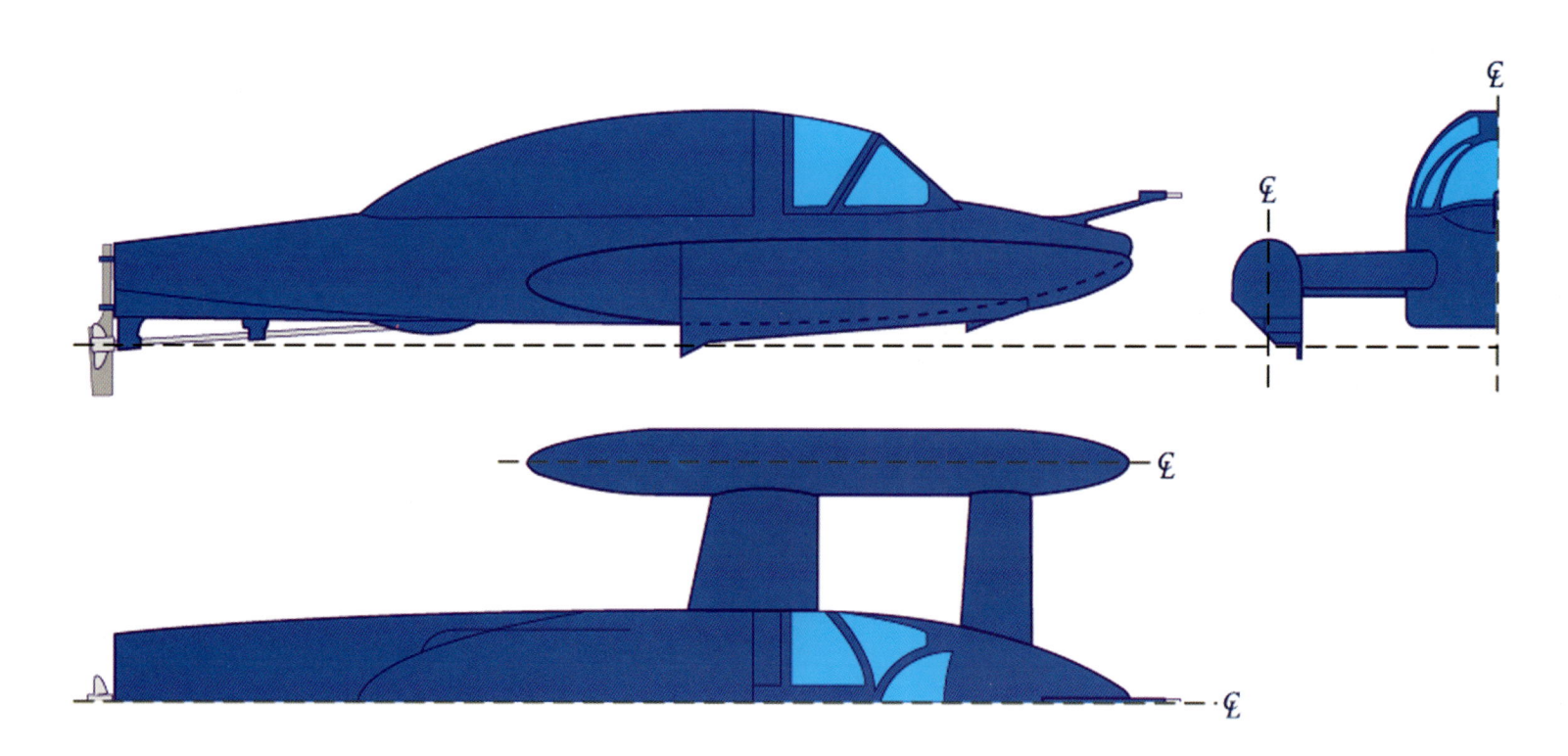

Prop-riding

By 1952 with 178.49 mph the fastest boat in the world was Slo-Mo-Shun IV, piloted by Stan Sayers. Designed by Ted Jones, a powerboat racer himself and a supervisor at the Boeing aircraft factory, Slo-Mo-Shun was a developed hydroplane of the Ventnor configuration, powered by an Allison 2,000 hp aero engine driving a two-bladed propeller at 11,500 revs per minute. Prop-riding is a method of semi-submerged propeller propulsion. At high speed the stern of the craft and the top blade of the propeller lift clear of the water, the propeller boss becoming the third point of support. Its use provides a gain of 20% over a fully submerged propeller by substantially reducing the drag, and the method does not create a loss of thrust at speeds in excess of 100 mph.

Ventnor

The previous record-breaking boats had all been of the Three Point Ventnor Configuration: two planing surfaces forward and one aft, driven by piston engines and propellers. In the case of Donald's 1949 Bluebird K4, the aft planing surface was the underneath of the transom, and for Slo-Mo-Shun it was the boss of the propeller. The boat shapes were very similar in design to previous three-point hydroplanes featuring a wide deck and bottom; this design resulted in flat-shaped hulls with high lift properties which had severe aerodynamic limitations, further increased by efforts of streamlining to reduce the frontal area.

These hydroplanes were operating on the very edge of stability, in fact literally trying to fly close to the water's surface between the volatile hydrodynamic and aerodynamic forces called Surface Effects. As these crafts centre of lift was forward of their centre of gravity they had the tendency to pitch-up and the faster they travelled the more this tendency increased, until the upward lift force became greater than the downward weight force causing them to overturn backwards. Slo-Mo-Shun, during one of the Gold Cup races, flipped over on her back ejecting Sayers whilst making a complete loop.

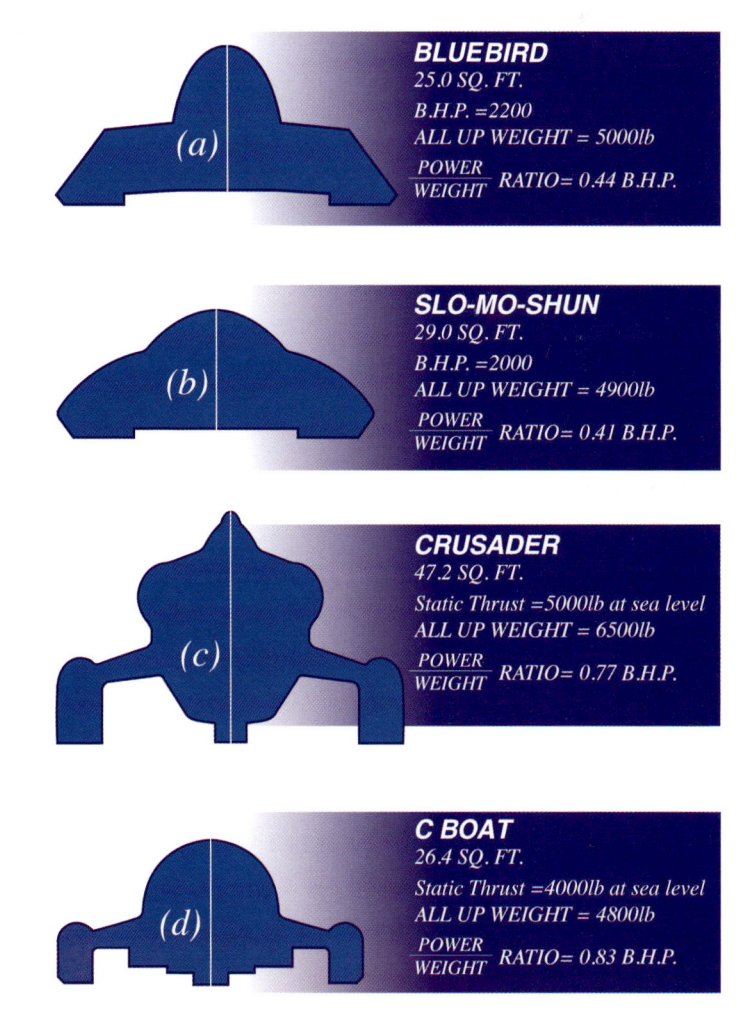

BLUEBIRD
Density = 11.5 LB/CU. FT. Volume

SLO-MO-SHUN
Density = 12.2 LB/CU. FT. Volume

CRUSADER
Density = 8.95 LB/CU. FT. Volume

C BOAT
Density = 14.7 LB/CU. FT. Volume

(a) **BLUEBIRD**
25.0 SQ. FT.
B.H.P. = 2200
ALL UP WEIGHT = 5000lb
$\frac{POWER}{WEIGHT}$ RATIO = 0.44 B.H.P.

(b) **SLO-MO-SHUN**
29.0 SQ. FT.
B.H.P. = 2000
ALL UP WEIGHT = 4900lb
$\frac{POWER}{WEIGHT}$ RATIO = 0.41 B.H.P.

(c) **CRUSADER**
47.2 SQ. FT.
Static Thrust = 5000lb at sea level
ALL UP WEIGHT = 6500lb
$\frac{POWER}{WEIGHT}$ RATIO = 0.77 B.H.P.

(d) **C BOAT**
26.4 SQ. FT.
Static Thrust = 4000lb at sea level
ALL UP WEIGHT = 4800lb
$\frac{POWER}{WEIGHT}$ RATIO = 0.83 B.H.P.

Three classes of water craft

Boats by definition are water-borne vessels that can be divided into three categories:

1. low-speed craft usually of the displacement type where water forces are predominant and air forces are negligible.
2. high-speed water craft usually of the planing type where water and air forces are of the same order.
3. high-speed water craft which eventually take off due to the predominance of air forces.

Class 1 craft are stabilised by water forces.

Class 2 craft must of necessity under normal operating conditions pass through class 1 and having reached class 2 because of their shape limitations must rely on water forces for stabilisation, air forces being un-stabilising.

Class 3 craft which must pass through classes 1 and 2 include those that are class 2 craft operating beyond their safe top speed and can fly as well as a cement brick, or aircraft, such as flying boats, using water as a means for take-off with aerodynamic lifting surfaces.

The regulations governing the water speed record in 1953 placed restrictions on design; an air rudder was allowed, but no aerodynamic lifting or control surfaces could be used, restricting any shape of potential record-breaking craft, so that to fly in a stable manner was not possible. Craft attempting the unlimited water speed record, for safety reasons, must remain in class 1 or 2.

Initial layout – C boat

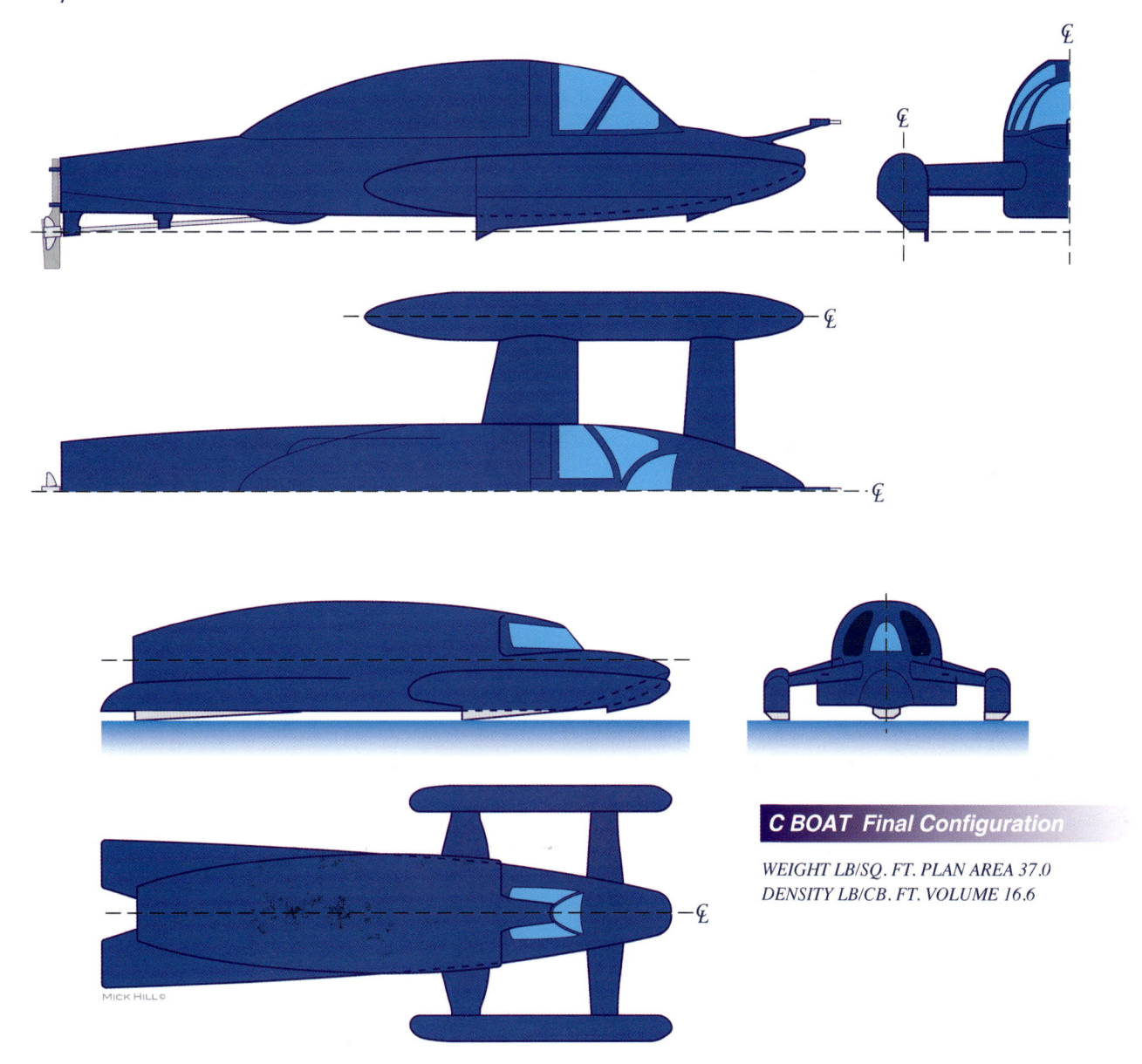

C BOAT Final Configuration

WEIGHT LB/SQ. FT. PLAN AREA 37.0
DENSITY LB/CB. FT. VOLUME 16.6

In compliance with the Harmsworth Trophy regulations, the Norris brothers designed a hydroplane for a crew of two with an enclosed cockpit in front of the engine compartment, both being situated in an aerodynamically safe central hull designed for speeds up to 200 mph. Above the cockpit canopy a ram air intake protruded for the supercharger.

From the outset the Norris design differed from all previous hydroplanes: they had cut out the kite surface between the forward planing surfaces and main hull to reduce lift. The planing surfaces or shoes were outrigged on spars and mounted on adjustable, detachable floats, which each contained an 18-gallon fuel tank. Two sets of floats were envisaged: a set for racing and another for speed records. The design was a prop-rider of about 5,000 lb driven by a 3,000 hp Rolls-Royce 37-litre Griffon engine with special sprint fuel, with the propellor spinning at 18,000 revolutions per minute.

67

Model tests

Once the preliminary 'C' boat design was completed, Saunders-Roe were asked to assess and test the Norris brothers' concept. Models were built for use in a programme of wind tunnel, water tank and radio-controlled tests. The wind tunnel tests, at a velocity of 100 feet per sec, were followed by towing tank experiments of 40 feet per second. Particular attention was paid to the transition stage between displacement and planing.

A scale model was dynamically corrected and fitted with a hydrogen peroxide cold rocket producing a static thrust of 6 lb for 25 seconds. Experiments started in May and were conducted on a wide expanse of sheltered water near Osborne. The rocket engine was charged with nitrogen pressurised to 2,000 lb to the square inch and hydrogen peroxide. Two radio controlled servos were mounted in the aft section of the model, one operating the rudder and the other triggering an emergency device comprising a deflector plate to close the rocket venturi.

Initial runs were of short duration, being designed to check the transitional period from displacement to planing and to enable spray patterns to be observed, filmed and photographed. The second series of tests dealt with stability in disturbed water and runs were made both across and downwind. The response to 0.5 to 1.25-inch model scale waves was surprisingly good.

The third series of tests involved rudder trials. A tapering wedge dagger plate rudder was mounted on the transom and offset from the centre line to port. Experiments were carried out with a rudder movement of 0 to 5 degrees either way and the results were very satisfactory.

The final trials dealt with maximum performance and stability, the runs were photographed and filmed and the timing was carried out by means of three synchronised stopwatches over a 100-yard course marked out by three timing posts. The maximum speed recorded was 87 mph.

After several runs and many crashes, the model finally hit the bank at over 80 mph and was destroyed. The explosion of the gas and aluminium tanks could be heard miles away. The tests had proved that the design was sound and could achieve a speed in excess of 200 mph.

Prop to jet

During the 'C' boat tests the news that Cobb had been killed in Crusader on Loch Ness at about the 240 mark was announced and it seemed with his death that the American looked like holding onto the record for the foreseeable future. It came as no surprise to Leo when Donald told him that he had sold his shareholding in Kiné to his partners the Meldrum brothers and that they were after the water speed record again. By the way, Lew and Ken married the Meldrum brothers' sisters.

A further assessment of propeller propulsion would have incurred significant design and development costs. Bearing in mind the speed limitations of the prop-rider, the small margin by which the record could be increased and the technical problems for such a craft, the new choice of power for the task fell to the jet engine. The new Bluebird would be at the leading edge of technology and succeed where both Malcolm and Cobb had failed.

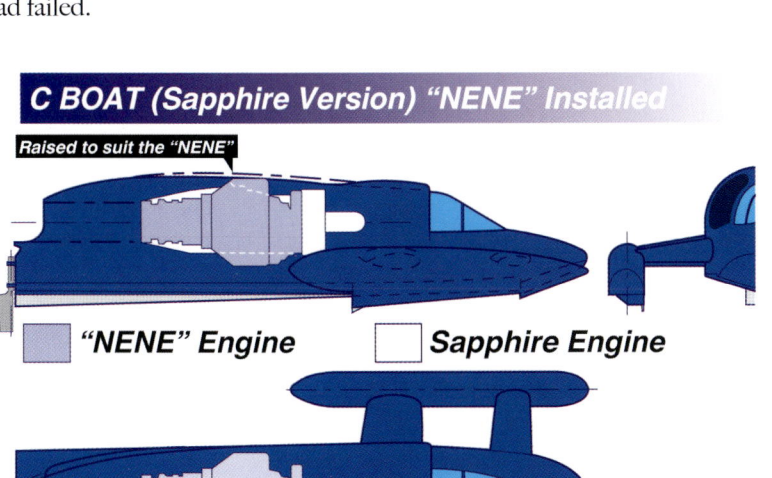

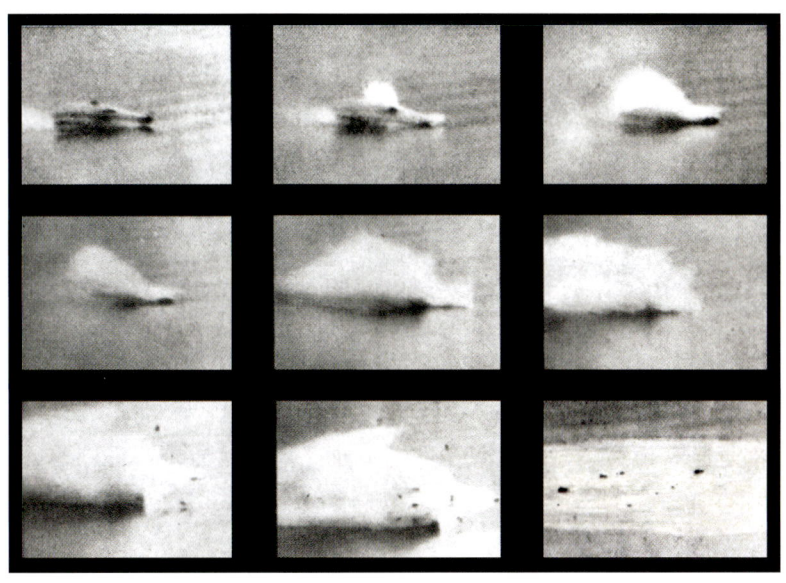

The last few 16 mm frames showing Crusader's break-up.

From a design point of view this resulted in further refinement of the hull and float design, with the basic configuration remaining unchanged, though mechanically much simplified. As soon as the final shape was defined more model tests were undertaken and the resulting performance calculations showed a potential calm water speed of 233 to 283 mph depending on the final size and weight of the craft. This was Saunders-Roe's last involvement with the project, the company declined to become involved in any further tests or the construction of a jet boat for corporate reasons.

Beryl

The Beryl jet engine was chosen as two were made available through an old friend of father's and Reid Railton, Air Commodore F.R. Banks, and the Ministry of Supply. A third unit was lent by the College of Aeronautics, Cranfield. Known just as Rod Banks he was one of the most experienced men in the aviation industry (he had worked out the best type of fuel for use in the Rolls-Royce R Schneider Cup engines, the same fuel used in the Bluebird cars and boats). The Metropolitan-Vickers Electrical Company overhauled and serviced all three units free of charge and provided the technicians to instruct Leo and Donald how to service and run the Beryl.

Once the project started to gain momentum backing came from firms such as Joseph Lucas electricals, Smiths Instruments Ltd, Block Tube Controls, Dunlop, Burman & Sons, Ultra Electrics and Birmid Industries, to name but a few, and at this point Accles & Pollock agreed to construct the hydroplane's main space frame free of charge.

The new Bluebird was wholly based on aircraft technology and there was not a boat builder in Great Britain that wanted to become involved with its construction. If it had been a conventional three-point hydroplane, any number of boat builders would have taken it on, but the moment it was designed to be built all in metal with a jet engine, nobody wanted to know.

The deal

David Nations was the British National Water Skiing Team coach and a close friend of Donald's. He had his club nautique at Ruislip Lido, west of London, of which Sir Wavell Wakefield was a member. It was on one of his visits that Nations introduced Sir Wavell to the idea that Campbell was looking for somebody to build the new Bluebird. However, it was some months before he approached Sir Wavell personally, cap-in-hand, to get her built. Sir Wavell was a director of Samlesbury Engineering in Lancashire, the engineering wing of the Lancashire Aircraft Company. After the initial contact he put much pressure on Samlesbury to get Bluebird built. It took three meetings in London before they even agreed to consider it and meet Donald.

At the last meeting the general manager of Samlesbury told Sir Wavell, 'What do you expect us to do? We build buses and trains. My lads have never built a boat in their lives.' But of course they were involved in the construction of aircraft wings and fuselage doors and for seventy-two long hours, Don, Lew and Ken did not know whether they would build the boat or not. Then, late the following night, Sir Wavell rang Donald at home and told him to get to the works; they want to see the plans. Within an hour Donald was off in the Aston and sitting outside the general manager's office at 7.30 the following morning. John Smith was very impressed with the accuracy of the drawings prepared by Norris Brothers. 'Yes my lads can do this. No problem at all.'

Donald Campbell and David Nations at Cyprus Gardens, Florida, in a celebrity charity event.

Final tests

Meanwhile Lew and Ken had been working around the clock on final designs and tests with the definitive model. Wind tunnel experiments were conducted in the 5 feet x 4 feet facility at the Imperial College of Science and Technology, in London's South Kensington, under the supervision of Professor Tom Fink.

The reduction of air-lift surfaces forward reduced the water-lift surfaces which could keep the craft from rising onto its planing points. It was decided to favour high-speed safety and to incorporate steps and flow directors to guarantee planing with reduced forward surfaces. In the test tank planing occurred at about 40 mph but the spray thrown up at this stage caused considerable concern. These problems would have to be overcome during trials with the full-size craft.

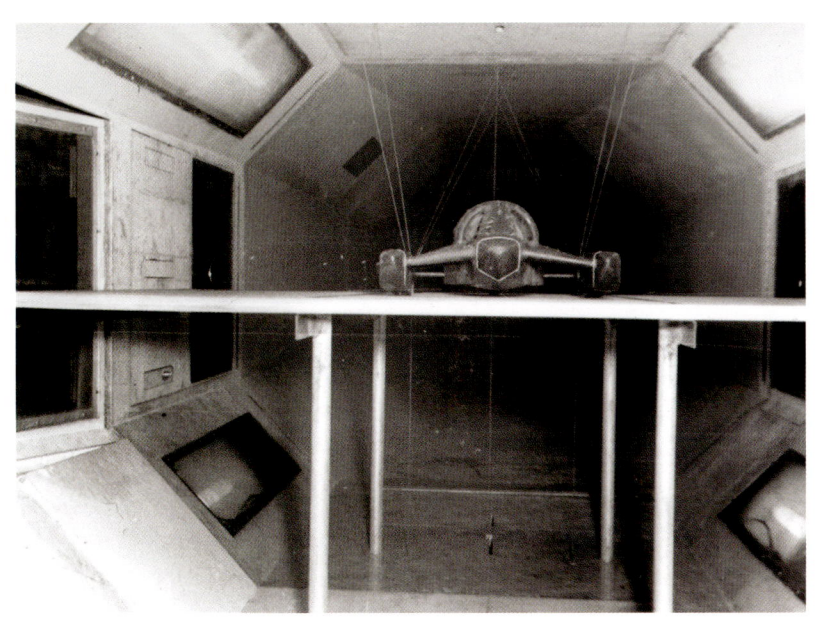

Dynamic stability

What was evident was that special precautions would be required for the new Bluebird to survive under such conditions. As no information was available to the Norris brothers concerning planing surfaces at the high speeds envisaged, the following methods of approach were used and built into the new Bluebird hydroplane:

Careful full-scale experimentation was essential and involved considerable risk to Donald; therefore, to ensure that the stability characteristics could be accurately determined, on-board instruments were fitted to measure pitch, roll, nose displacement, vertical acceleration and speed, and transmitted to a shore base and recorded for analysis.

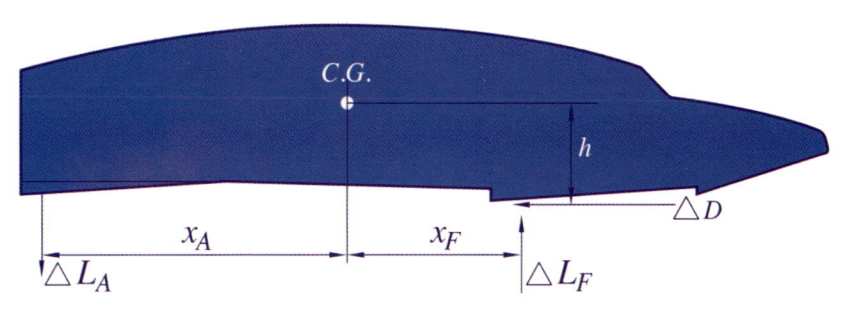

Structure

General rigidity was considered essential; any deflections of the structure could affect the rudder due to increased control circuit stiffness and could also result in unacceptable changes of incidence to the planing surfaces.

Once the space frame was completed by Accles & Pollock, it was delivered to the main constructors, Samlesbury Engineering in Blackburn, Lancashire. The frame was manufactured in high-tensile T60 2 inches square tubular steel and consisted of the main load-bearing members with two transverse spars of high-duty aluminium alloy running through the whole length of the main hull for the attachment of the forward planing surfaces. 'Pick-up' holes were provided by small round tubes welded into the main square sections for the main spars, engine mountings and rudder brackets. The frame was watertight throughout.

The main forward spars to which the floats were attached were fabricated from light alloy watertight box-sections of exceptional strength, self-supporting if immersed in water. The spars were connected to the main frame and outer planes with high tensile steel bolts to facilitate their removal for transport.

High-grade, non-corrosive light alloys, developed for marine craft, were used in the manufacture of the hull and some 70,000 rivets were utilised throughout the whole of the craft. Birmid Industries supplied the Birmabright light alloy steel used in the main skin, which was attached to the frame by a variety of special rivets. Watertightness was achieved by lapping, welding and the use of sealing compounds. The skin was supported by cross-panels, riveted to steel plates which in turn were welded to the steel frame. All the skin and panels below the waterline were permanent and, above, were removable in two sections allowing access to the engine compartment. The whole assembly was stress carrying: the main frame carried the direct vertical acceleration, deceleration and skid loads. The resulting torsional loads were carried by the skin and sub-structure.

The floats consisted of watertight light alloy box sections fabricated from angles and sheeting with the anti-dive surfaces incorporated in the structure. The three main planing shoes, machined from solid light alloy billets, were bolted onto the floats and main hull. These surfaces were stressed to stand up to 600 lb per square inch. High tensile steel directional stabilising fins were attached to the forward planing shoes with counter-sunk steel screws.

The flat underside of the central hull was designed to withstand the severe stresses that would be imposed at high speed and was built from reinforced corrugated light alloy sheets joined together with some 10,000 rivets.

Fuel tank

Because of the limited space and the necessity of keeping the fuel tank above the centre of gravity (CG), a 48 gallon ring tank or saddle tank was incorporated with the air intakes passing directly through its middle. The vertical CG of the tank was high when full; however, the main advantage was that, as the tank, emptied, it was self-balancing and did not alter the craft's CG or angle of attack, which is of paramount importance when running at ultra-high speed.

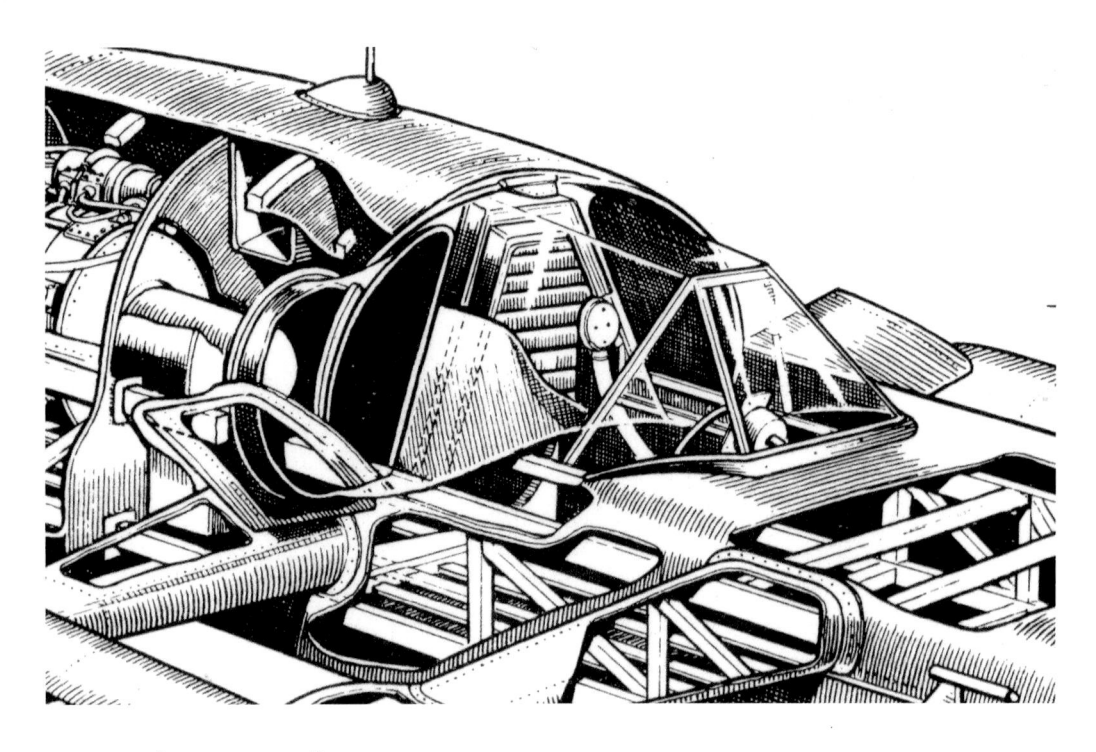

Steering, cockpit, controls and instrumentation

The wind tunnel tests showed quite clearly that the craft would be aerodynamically directionally unstable and at this stage no provision was made to fit a tail fin. The alternative was to incorporate underwater stabilising fins fitted on the inside edge of the forward planing surfaces. These being liable to damage from semi-submerged objects, the fins were swept back and sharpened to a razor's edge. To the rear an offset, fully turning stabilised fin was used as a rudder. It consisted of a straight wedge section controlled by a tiller arm coupled to a conventional steering box and wheel through aircraft type control rods.

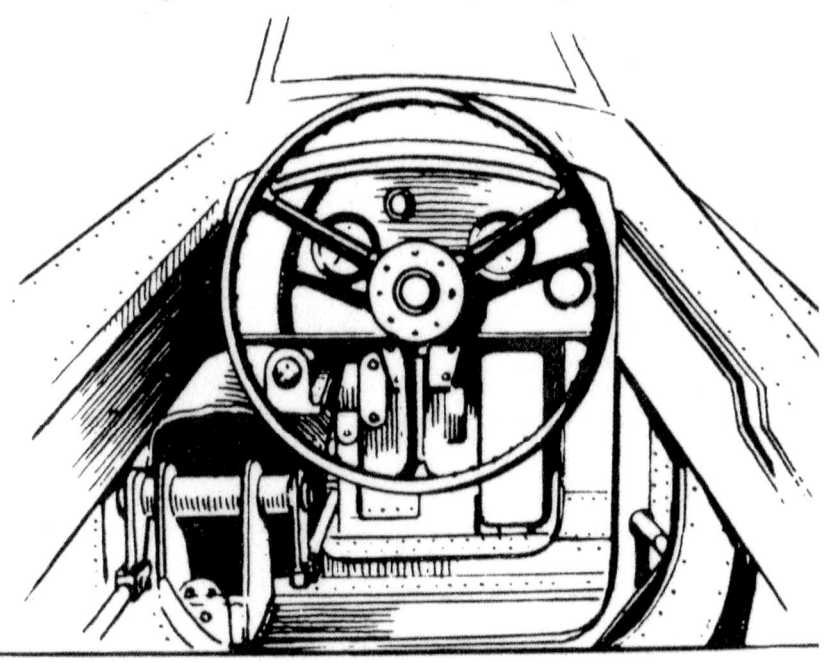

The two main controls were the steering wheel and the foot-operated throttle. In addition there were high and low-pressure fuel cut-off levers. The instruments, which were supplied by Smiths Instruments, consisted of an air-speed indicator, revolution counter, fuel pressure gauge, jet pipe temperature gauge and G meter with a maximum hand. The radio telephone was controlled by a simple on-off switch, and was supplied and fitted by Ultra Electric.

The pilot's seat was built into the main frame and the back cushioning was attached to the bulkhead immediately forward of the main spar. Dunlop supplied an air-cushioned Dunlopillo seat with a safety harness. In the event of a sinking at low speed, a 30-minute air supply was available.

The cockpit canopy was made of aluminium with Perspex windows. A hand-operated wiper was used to clear away any low-speed spray on the forward window. The air intakes were to the rear and on either side of the cockpit. The compartment behind the pilot's head formed a streamlined fairing between the two ducts and housed the electronic telemetry instrumentation.

Detailed design of the Bluebird started in January and she was officially handed over to the Bluebird team on 26th November 1954 by Mr Eric Rylands, chairman and managing director of Samlesbury, and was unveiled by Lady Wakefield. The whole project had cost in excess of £25,000, without counting the cost of the engines, materials and labour provided which had been free of charge.

MR DONALD CAMPBELL'S TURBO-JET HYDROPLANE "BLUEBIRD"
Main Constructors-Samlesbury Engineering Limited.

75

Ullswater 1955

It was on a freezing day in February 1955 that Dorothy broke a bottle of champagne against an iron bar fixed against the bows of the Bluebird as she sat on the slipway at Ullswater in the Lake District. 'I name this boat Bluebird', she said, repeating the very same words I had used myself when I launched Father's boat 16 years before in 1939 on Coniston. 'May God bless her, her pilot and all who work with her.' I stepped into the cockpit and Bluebird was towed out to the centre of the lake as I prepared myself for the first run in a high-speed hydroplane since the old Bluebird sank four years earlier. The difference this time was I knew the water barrier was waiting just ahead.

Cliff Polley ready to help Donald Campbell.

On the pier with Tom Fink, the timekeepers and Leo.

From the moment Bluebird had been launched we were in trouble; on the very first run the bow, instead of rising, had dived under the surface like a submarine and waves had cascaded over the cockpit and into the air intakes putting out the jet engine.

We worked around the clock to try to make her come up onto the plane, even hanging a quarter of a ton of lead on the stern, but to no avail. As we were to prove time and time again, Lew and Ken Norris' design was superlative: all their ingenuity had gone into building a craft capable of surviving the tremendous hammering of speeds in excess of 250 mph and a shape that would not turn on its back at speeds approaching 300. However by February 1955 we were doing barely 7 mph, whilst experiencing the diving phenomenon. Leo fitted aluminium sheets between the floats and hull to stop spray and water entering the engine.

On 11th March, Father's birthday, I climbed into the cockpit, closed the cover, lit the engine and put my foot down, increasing the power gently; suddenly the nose began to lift smoothly, the stern came up, Bluebird levelled off and was off like a rocket; the acceleration was terrific. I was up to 100 in no time at all and almost ran out of lake. Ken, Lew and the whole team were totally elated, but the question now was, how we get Bluebird up to speed without the hardware between the spars?

A few weeks later I found myself up a stepladder in the middle of the muddy duck pond at Abbotts with my Bolex in hand, whilst Leo and Maurie Parfitt, his number two, were towing a scale wooden model of Bluebird across the pond on a line attached to an electric pulley on the bankside.

The model tests I filmed in slow motion from the top of the ladder and processed the thousands of feet black and white stock in my bathroom and dried it in the orangery. The living room became our laboratory and Dorothy cheerfully put up with the upheaval to the domestic routine and fed us at all hours of the day and night. The only thing that mattered was the water speed record; after two weeks we had got nowhere.

One day we moved the spars up that were supporting the floats and realised that as the boat went forward they were being sucked under and throwing the water over the tops of the spars, dragging the bow down under the surface. This left the Norris brothers the task of redesigning the whole front end and moving up the spars. By July we had completed the modifications and were ready to go! As I put my foot down the bow came up easily and she was away.

On 15th July we reached 180 mph on Ullswater and I decided to call in the timekeepers. Leo asked me if I was being a little hasty and I told him no, we were down to our last £300. The other problem I had was the nagging pain in my back from an old injury playing rugby, made worse by the experience of racing on Garda for the Oltranza Cup in 1951. The pain ran down my back and the length of my leg. I was playing a game of chess on the morning of 23rd July when Chris Coley ran into the room to inform me that Leo had radioed from the middle of the lake to say that conditions were perfect to have a go. We made our way to the pier where Bluebird was already launched and Maurie Parfitt helped me into the cockpit. 'How's the back Skipper?' 'Don't ask Maurie, bloody agony,' I replied, as I closed the cockpit cover and started up the Beryl jet engine. I let her idle her way along in the bay and then put my foot down and taxied towards the centre of the lake and the beginning of the course; as I started to put the power on the Beryl began to scream and as the nose came up we were away like a rocket. It flashed; I saw Dad in his Slipper, the frustration on his lined face, my old friend Cobb and the Italian powerboat ace Mario Verga … they had all failed in the face of the barrier.

78

Bugger it! Here we go and down went my foot. Bluebird was running flat level now and gently vibrating from sponson to sponson, tramping, as we shot-off down the lake: 180 – 190 – 200 – 220, the air speed indicator went off the clock, take it easy old boy ... leave some for later. I was commenting furiously over the radio, but no one heard me: the force of the air at speed had broken the aerial. The red buoys marking the end of the kilometer flashed past as I eased off the throttle gently. I had no idea of what speed I had reached and at the end of the course I refuelled, Robin Brown gave me a glass of lemonade and the news came over the radio that I'd cracked 200. It was an overcast morning, heavy and grey, typical of the Lakes. A breeze was starting to blow and the surface of the water began to ripple; there was no time to waste. I made the return run, keeping her steady at 190. It was much choppier this time and I almost had my insides shaken out.

This would be more than good enough with the run down. I cut the power and started to drift towards the end of the lake and the pier. Leo's white launch with his son Tim at the helm was speeding towards me and I could see him waving even 500 yards off I could see him beaming and I knew we had done it. It was one of the most extraordinary moments of my life. They came alongside and Leo clambered aboard and gave me a hug. 'Bloody fine show Don!' After all the strain we had been through both of us broke down and cried like a couple of kids. We had worked so hard for the last six years to get this damned, bloody record and all of a sudden we'd finally got it! 202.3 mph. We had penetrated the water barrier.

Lewis, Kenneth, Donald and Leo.

The whole team was physically and mentally exhausted and all I wanted to do was get away from it all so I headed down to the South of France and had my first real holiday in over three years. One night I received a phone call from Leo telling me that my US representative, Commander Edwin Ferris, had signed a deal with Mobil Oil Company and a certain Harry Sloan in Las Vegas, who was the PR for the Sahara Hotel and its owner Milton Prell. We were going to make an attempt on the water speed record on Lake Mead in Nevada, which was just outside Las Vegas, during the season of unlimited hydroplane races that the hotel had organised to draw attention to the area as a centre for water sports. Mobil Oil would provide financial support, against advertising rights with an appropriate bonus, fuel and lubricants.

Don with the two Dorothys, receiving stereo nagging.

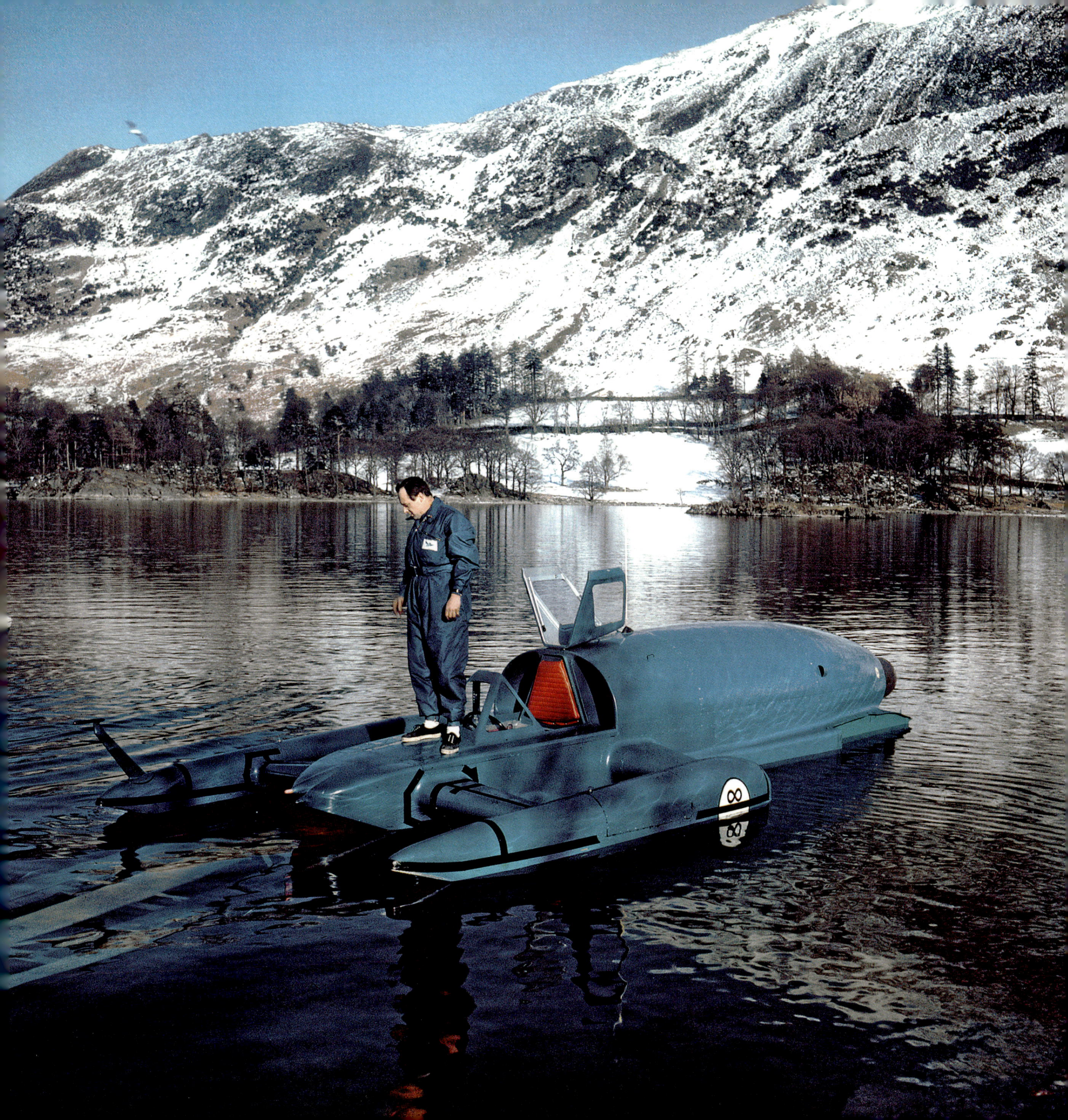

FAST & LOOSE
1955–1959

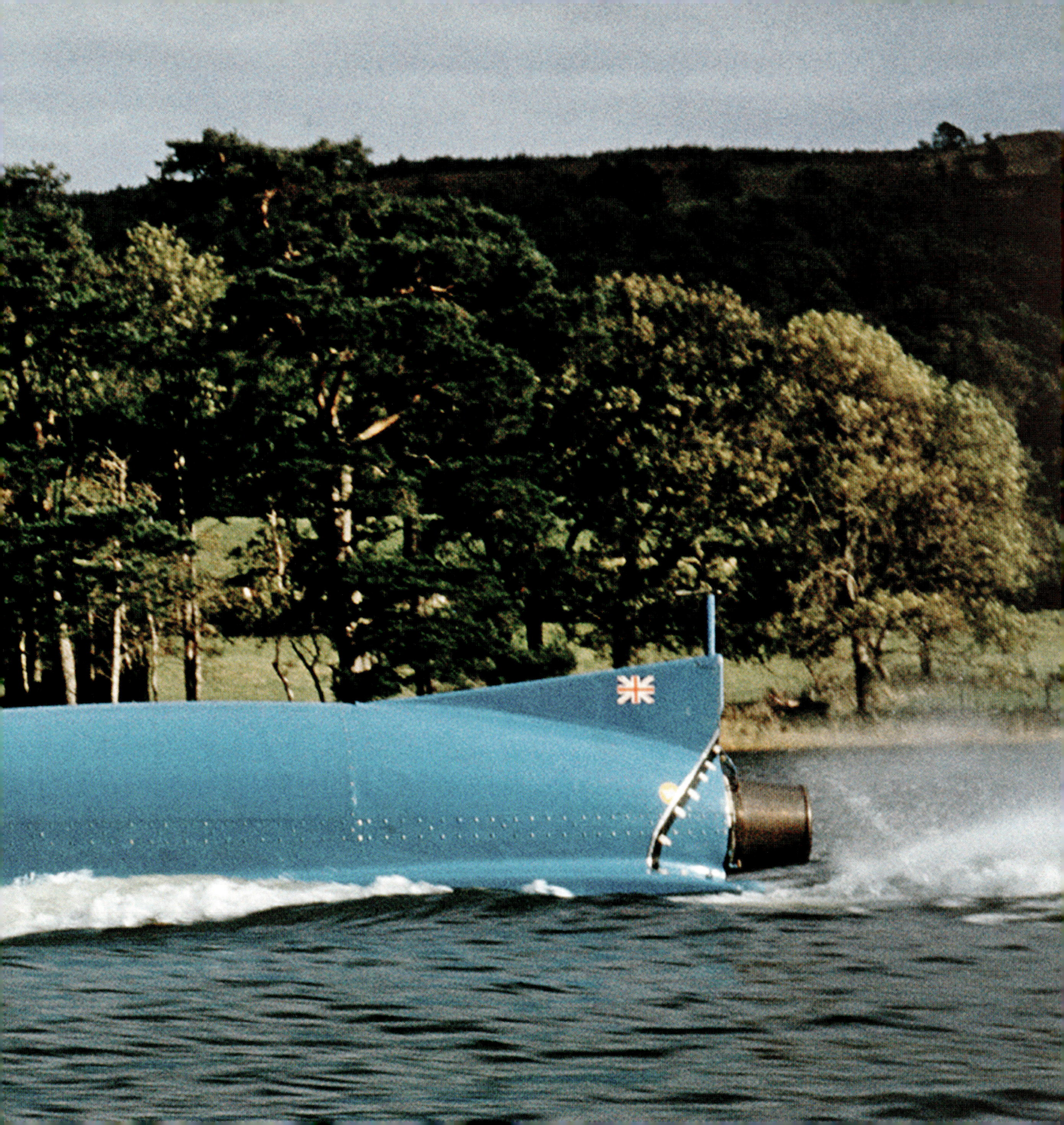

LAS VEGAS – NEVADA 1955

Donald with his 16 mm Kodak movie camera and 35 mm Stereo Realist on board the USS United States in New York Harbour with his United States' representative Commander Edwin Ferris.

Kenneth St Oegger, unlimited hydroplane champion chats with Donald Campbell in front of Henry Kaiser's Haiwaii Kai.

The Racket Club at Harbour Island.

Matty Banks, Hollywood's foremost plastic surgeon with Donald Campbell.

Peggy.

The problem we had was that the agreement hinged on the team making the attempt on 15th October, live on network coast-to-coast television for a programme called *The Wide, Wide World* on NBC. It was said to have an audience of 60 million. 'Balls', said Leo. 'Do you have any idea of the chances of conditions being right on the lake, on that day and at the right time. Forget it brother.' 'I know...I know,' I said, 'but we can't pull out now.' We both knew it would probably be hopeless, but to retract would have looked bad on the team and on Britain as a major high-speed player. I decided to take a chance. We had but three weeks to prepare the Bird. The team left for Mead on a transporter plane across the Atlantic with Bluebird, having had her floats removed and all our equipment via New York. Three weeks later I joined the Boys in the Sahara Hotel which was our headquarters during the attempt.

Lake Mead was 30 miles away from Vegas and looked like a crater in the middle of the moon: 300 miles square of deep blue water set amongst towering mountains. Formed by damming the Colorado River, there are a number of reaches and the country is pretty rough and wild, mostly scrubby desert. The course selected for us lay in a western reach about 17 miles long, running north to south. In the north we could see a line of islands and the great water tower that feeds Las Vegas. To the south were mountains.

The measured mile was laid out opposite a landmark called Burro Point, 7 or 8 miles from our boathouse at the end of the only road from town. Our refuelling point was a raft near an island beyond the end of the course. Our base was in the state of Nevada and the refuelling point was in the state of Arizona. A barrage balloon was flying to mark the start of the course; but the surroundings were so vast it was dwarfed so that it was almost invisible.

The Sahara Hotel was lush in a way that only an American hotel could be; it has every amenity any holidaymaker or gambler could possibly desire: gift shops and barbers, tailors and night clubs. Obviously the casino and the tables are the main attraction: roulette, blackjack and craps, or any number of weird and wonderful one-armed bandits or other gambling devices. Every night, from 6 p.m. until 7 the following morning, there is continuous entertainment on stage, and usually three different types of bands.

We were due to make our first run at 1 p.m. plus 4 minutes and 20 seconds!

The lake authority had cleared the area of all vessels from 10 a.m. onwards that Sunday morning. In fact boats of all sizes and descriptions had turned up and they seemed to carry on appearing from the heart of the desert as if by magic. There must have been about 400 of them. Leo started to look increasingly worried and just exploded, 'Bugger this. It's bloody stupid. What are we, a damned circus act? It's bloody hopeless Don, just hopeless.' The wash from the combined spectator craft had produced a long and heavy oily swell.

I hit the beginning of the course at 4 minutes past one and 16 seconds. Bluebird got up to speed and would have done credit to Buffalo Bill and any Wild West Bronco Show. The speed for the run was 167 mph. I refuelled 17 miles away from base and, meanwhile, I was interviewed on a radio programme from the cockpit. I made the return run in slightly better conditions and stopped in the designated area for close-up shots of Bluebird! The show was over and the spectator craft started to move around; they were chased by police launches which made the matters worse. Little by little the wash started to overcome Bluebird.

One of the team came alongside in a support boat to put on the cover over the jet nozzle and he burnt his hand. The cover went 100 feet to the bottom. As Bluebird was towed back her stern went lower and lower until she too gently slid below the waves. Then I had to swim for it and someone hauled me out of the water too stunned to speak. Suddenly Bluebird's nose broke the surface like some weird prehistoric monster. Don Woolley went over the side of the big cruiser with a heavy rope and tied it round Bluebird's front spar. In seconds she was gone again and settled on the bottom.

For the next 11 hours divers worked without break with tackle, chains, blocks and ropes from the stern of two big cruisers. Bit by bit we inched her up to the surface again. At 1.30 the next morning Bluebird was back on dry land. She was very badly damaged: the engine was full of silt. The water was particularly corrosive and all the boat's bright aluminium parts had become a dull black. As we hauled her back into the tent that served as a boathouse we heard a Yank say, 'Let's see the suckers get out of this one then …'

Colonel Roberts.

Leo and Peter Carr at Nellis.

88

We needed facilities to work on Bluebird fast to save her flooded hull and the engine, so I set off for the United States Air Force Fighter School at Nellis Air Base, with an English officer that was stationed there and who had come to the lake to see our effort. I travelled the 15 minutes with Captain Peter Carr from Lake Mead to talk the base commander, Colonel Roberts. Peter convinced Colonel Roberts that it would be good US-UK public relations to raise Bluebird and then service it. It was thanks to Peter Carr that exactly one month after the sinking, Donald was able to break the World Water Speed Record.

The following fortnight was a blur of hard work. Bluebird was stripped right down. Now we reaped the value of the spares we had flown out from England, including a second jet engine, and we all worked tremendously hard. The engine was replaced, the instruments were stripped down together with the whole fuel system, control systems and the electronics. When everything was reassembled and Bluebird was herself again, we test started the engine and the Beryl ran perfectly. We were ready to move back to Lake Mead by 9th November. I was more determined than ever that we were going to have a new record as soon as possible.

Lakeside: preparing for a launch.

With singer Kay Martin.

Six days later there was a calm forecast and we were breakfasting at 4.30 a.m. in the Casbah Lounge of the Sahara. All around us were people playing blackjack, roulette and craps. On stage Kay Martin and her Bodyguards were beating out, 'I want a casting couch for Christmas,' a red-hot hit from her latest album. It really was a glittering setting and everything seemed somehow unreal; you expected Philippe Marlowe to appear from behind a bouncer. As we rose to go, Kay rushed down in skimpy attire from the stage and smacked a kiss on my lips, wishing me good luck. Leo remarked he hoped it was not like the black pussy outside Ascari's room ... I can't tell you what Clive said, Dad would have approved ...

Leo with Peggy and the hire car.

Leo, Maurie and Don Woolley.

90

On the slip.

We were delayed down by the water's edge by a dodgy connection in the timekeeper's wiring and then after by a missing official who had last been seen blind-drunk at a blackjack table in the Sands with a call girl on each arm. He duly arrived alone in the sheriff's car in the safekeeping of a deputy, resplendent in his Ray Bans, Stetson and Cuban heels. The whole bloody record was over quicker than you could say Ronald Ray Guns; the first run was made at 10.27 and by 10.42 it was all over – we had set a new water speed record of 216 mph, exactly a month to the day Bluebird had sunk. That night there was a tremendous celebration in the Sahara. The Chamber of Commerce presented me with an enormous gold cup and we had a party we would never forget.

A few days later I received a letter from the Foreign Office with congratulations for giving British prestige such a boost in what was regarded as a tough part of the world. My mind strayed back twenty years to Utah when Father had become the first man to do 300 mph on land at Bonneville. 'What can we do next Leo?' 'I don't know Don. But I'm bloody sure you're going to tell me what bee's in your over-imaginative bonnet.'

The owner of the Sahara Hotel, Milton Prell, with the newsreel and press boys.

Lake Mead, the slip, pier and marina.

NBC-TV coast-to-coast broadcast link for *The Wide, Wide World* programme.

93

My dear Leo a double! The land and water speed records in the same day old boy! Well knock off the land speed in the morning on Bonneville; hop over to Mead do the water speed in the afternoon ... just like that.

You're talking out of your bloody arse Skipper – it just took us six bloody years to get the water speed record and now the Speed King can do it in twelve hours.

Angels and ministers of grace, defend us!
Hamlet, Act 1, Scene 4

Don Woolley, Andrew Browm, Leo, Maurie, Cliff Polley and Donald the day after the record.

CHRISTMAS 1955

We were home in England a few days before Christmas, leaving Bluebird behind us in the States. As soon as Christmas was over, Donald went to see Lew and Ken to ask them about designing a car to beat John Cobb's post-war record of 394 mph. Ken jumped at the opportunity and went for it like a duck. They agreed to start developing a design if Donald would start looking for backers. Bluebird K7 had cost about £25,000; the car was to cost over £500,000. K7 had had about twenty firms involved; long before the Bluebird car took shape, more than eighty companies were involved at different levels. Donald was anxious to get back to Coniston to go after the Butlin Trophy and prize money. I stayed with the Norris brothers discussing the set-backs we had experienced at Lake Mead.

A friend of Donald's, Sir Billy Butlin, owner of the famous Butlin's holiday camp, put up £25,000 to encourage research in the field of record-breaking; as there was no one else in the field the money went to Donald on an annual basis. The sum was to be spread over five years; a sum of £5,000, plus a gold cup, would be awarded to anyone who beat a speed record in any one year, for the next five years. Several American boats, all prop-riders, were in the field for this award. Guy Lombardo, Ted Jones (designer of Slo-Mo-Shun) and Henry Kaiser's son were all planning to go after Donald's record and they did not stand a chance. K7 had undergone a few modifications with reduced trim aft, a replacement domed canopy of blown Perspex which slid forward on two runners, and a new set of modified spray deflectors.

Following our return, Donald learned he was being awarded the CBE. His reputation had never been higher, the post-war period of austerity was now a thing of the past, and Britain was entering a period which, according to the Conservative Party, we had never had it so good.

Leo Villa

Donald Campbell with Billy Butlin at Ruislip Lido. David Nations' Club Nautique in West London.

"We had never had it so good!"

CONISTON 1956

Donald was anxious to get back to Coniston to go after the Butlin prize money. I spent some time with the Norris brothers discussing improvements to Bluebird from the setbacks we had experienced at Lake Mead and by late summer we were back up at Coniston. The Norris brothers looked in on us during trials, as did Lady Campbell and Dorothy with Gina, who was attending her first record attempt. She called me Unc and from that time onwards the whole team called me Unc, but especially Donald.

On 19th September, after a misty morning, the surface seemed smooth and calm, the timekeepers were in position and Maurie was at the start. I was in my usual position in mid-lake. Donald was hoping to crack 250 mph on this attempt. We had discussed this the night before when he had told me that on the first north–south run, he proposed to feel his way around the 240 mph mark and if the water surface proved good, he would open Bluebird on the way back, and pick up the extra speed for an average of 250 mph. This was the first run at Coniston in the new jet-boat and Donald was a little doubtful about whether he would be able to slow the boat down in time.

I gave Donald the all-clear and he was soon underway. His usual commentary came over the radio telephone but as his speed increased, his voice became blurred and difficult to understand. He came by my boat at a terrific speed, the fastest yet as far as I could see, quite steady, but light on the bows. The port stabilising fin was clearly visible; this was the first time I had ever seen it, and it convinced me that the bows were coming up. He was soon out of sight, and as his speed dropped off his voice became more distinct. I heard him saying that the boat had gone crazy, something had broken, and he couldn't do a damn thing with it. 'I've taken a hell of a beating,' he said. Then, a few seconds later; 'I can see the refuelling boat. I'm going alongside now. Come in, Leo, give me my speed? 'While I was waiting for the speed to come in from the timekeepers, I warned him that the Bluebird was showing signs of being a bit light.

Leo Villa

NATIONAL SPORTING CLUB

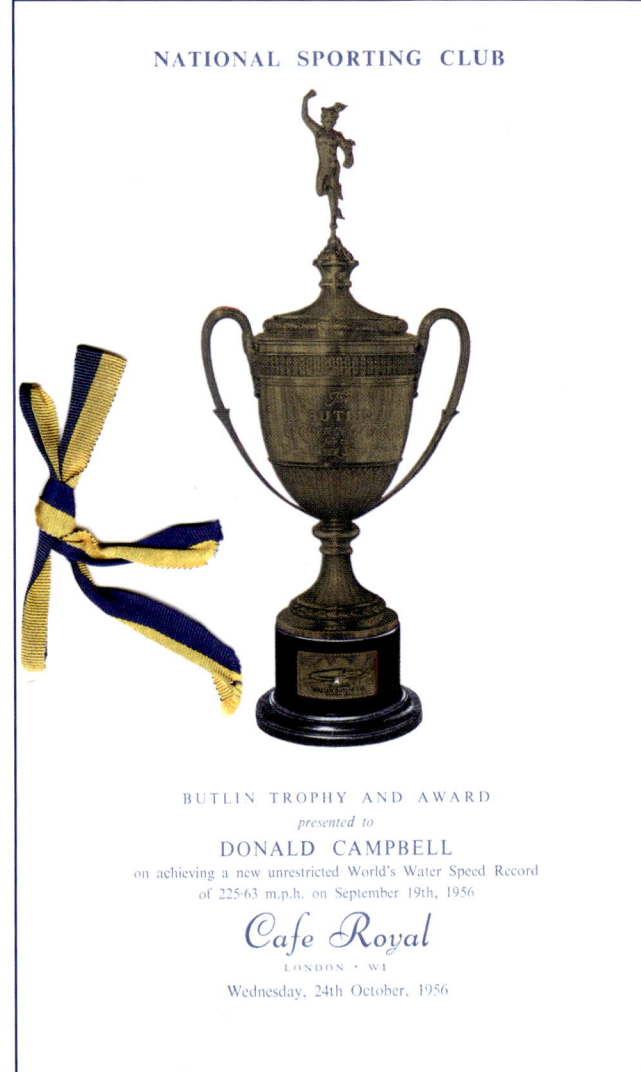

BUTLIN TROPHY AND AWARD
presented to
DONALD CAMPBELL
on achieving a new unrestricted World's Water Speed Record
of 225·63 m.p.h. on September 19th, 1956

Cafe Royal
LONDON · W1
Wednesday, 24th October, 1956

Then we got the speed: 286 mph. He wouldn't believe it. 'You're bloody mad!' His air speed indicator had recorded 240 mph, the envisaged speed. We allowed 20 minutes for his wash to die down and for the surface to settle and I gave him the all-clear for the return run. This time he passed us at a far more dignified pace. The new Perspex canopy had misted over, reducing visibility to almost nil, and fumes were now getting into the cockpit. The return run was made at a gentle speed of 164.48 mph, giving an average of 225.63 mph: a new record. Donald had proved yet again that he could handle Bluebird K7 at speed. Although he hadn't established the record he had intended, he became the first person to travel at more than 250 mph on the water, as well as the first contender to win the Butlin Trophy and the £5,000 that went with it.

Leo, the Skipper, and Leo's nephew Phil.

With Lew Norris and family.

Rex, Leo and Maurie with the Mobil boys.

100

At Abbotts.

Waiting for conditions.

CANANDAIGUA SNAPSHOT 1957

Canandaigua Lake Promotions, headed by Howard Samuels, Clifford Murphy and Sheppard Ford Automobile, decided to invite Campbell/Bluebird out onto their lake to make an attempt on the water speed record as a publicity stunt for their area in upstate New York. The lake and its amenities were the big attraction; it was about 350 miles from New York City off the East West Freeway. Canandaigua's prosperity had tumbled when a throughway was built to the north completely bypassing the town.

The idea was to turn an old showroom formerly used by the Sheppard Ford Automobile dealership into a Campbell Museum of Speed that would bring in the crowds. Profits from their takings would then be invested in a YMCA building fund. Apart from the display building, they had to build Bluebird Park with a car park, entrance gate and a slip straight down from the museum to the lake for Bluebird.

People entering the park could watch us working on the Bird. There was the spare Beryl engine on display, as well as Sir Malcolm's 350 hp Sunbeam and the R type from K4. They screened the Mobil movie made about our success on Lake Mead, The Challenge of the Lake, at regular intervals during the day.

Leo Villa

Report 2 from USS United States, 28th June 1957
Bluebird team members' designation made en route:

Leo Villa	Team Captain/Chief Engineer
Maurice Parfitt	Engineer, mechanical
John Fenn	Marine Consultant
Andrew Brown	Technical Director electronics
James Hinton	Course Master and Dunlop rep
Rex Pickering	British Admin and Public Relations
Cliff Poley	Designer's Technician (Stress Engineer)
Jeff Spencer	Engineer, electrical
Hazel Ottington	Personal Secretary

Loading K7 onto the Adams Brothers lorry at Abbotts for Southampton docks.

Maurie, John, Rex, Cliff, Jim, Andy, Gina, Hazel, Don and Joan.

Jim Hinton of Dunlops, Donald Campbell, Leo and Andy Brown.

Report 3 from NYC, 25th June 1957
Arrival New York harbor on liner USS United States with tremendous press, film and television coverage, as follows:

8.00 a.m.	Press interviews and pictures on board
8.20	Phone interview – Carroway – from room on pier
8.35	Film interview on board
9.15	John Tillman, filmed interview
9.30	Emil Fisher, film for Movietone
945	NBC filmed interview, Tom Flaherty
11.15	Leave boat
2.30 p.m.	Press interview
3.15	Fields
5.00	This is New York – CBS – taped interview
6.15	Dynamic Television
8.15	Tillman

Leo Villa, Jim Hinton, C. Poley, took Soconey plane up to Canandaigua to complete Bluebird preparations there. Parfitt, Spencer, and Pickering supervised unloading Bluebird and travelled up with her by road, causing a great deal of interest en route.

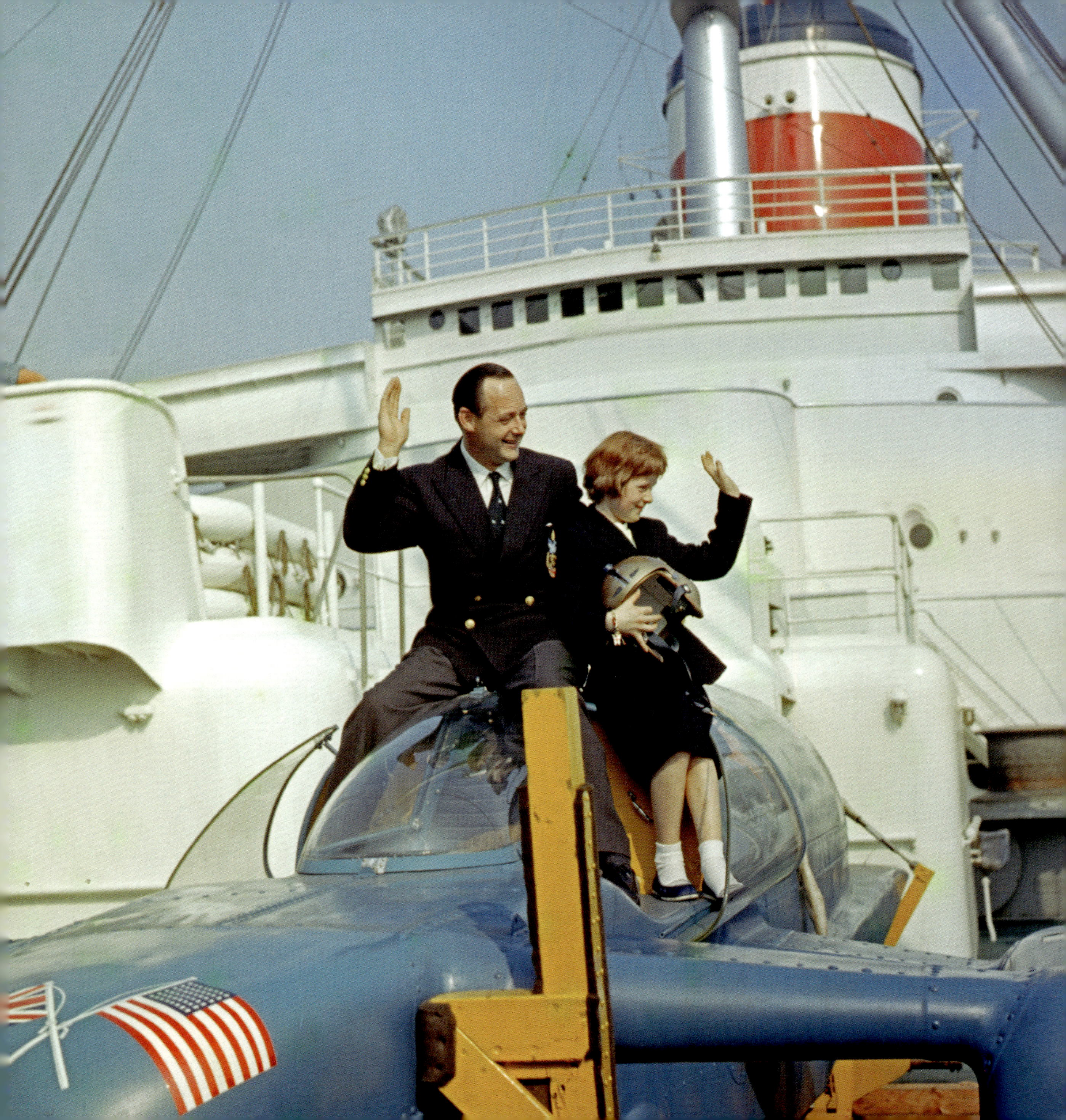

Wednesday 26th June 1957

8 a.m.   WINS telephone interview for Contact programme
9 a.m.   Personal interview with George Marshall of International News Service
1145 p.m.   Donald Campbell received by Mayor of New York and presented letter from the Mayor of London
                     Remainder of team travel to Canandaigua where Bluebird was installed in Bluebird Park

Parade of team, followed by opening of Bluebird Park – team all well and in excellent spirits.

Joan, Donald Campbell, Maurie, Gina and friend with Rex.

Pier head, Bluebird Park.

Saturday 29th June
Test run with Bluebird cancelled owing to rough water.

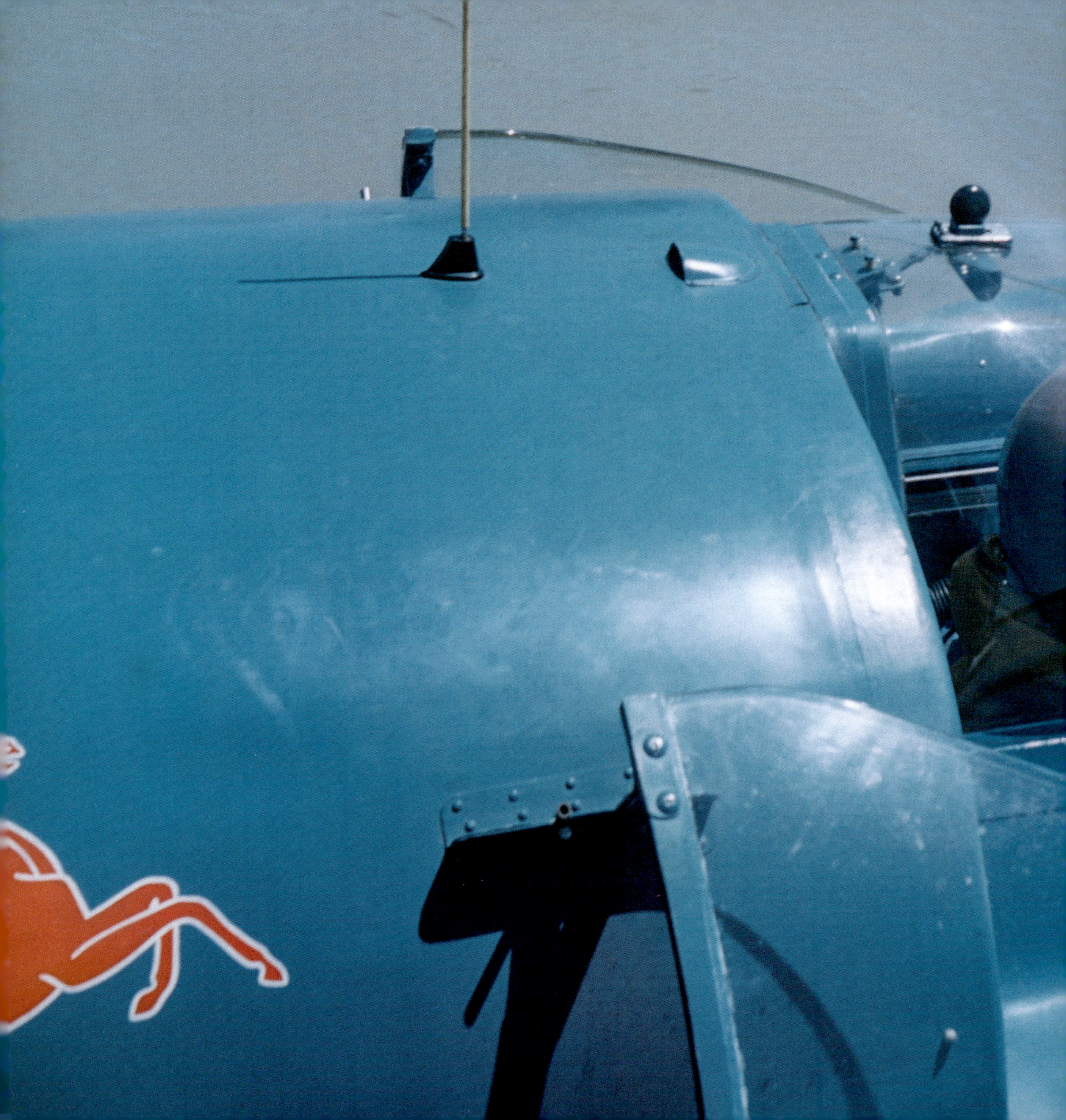

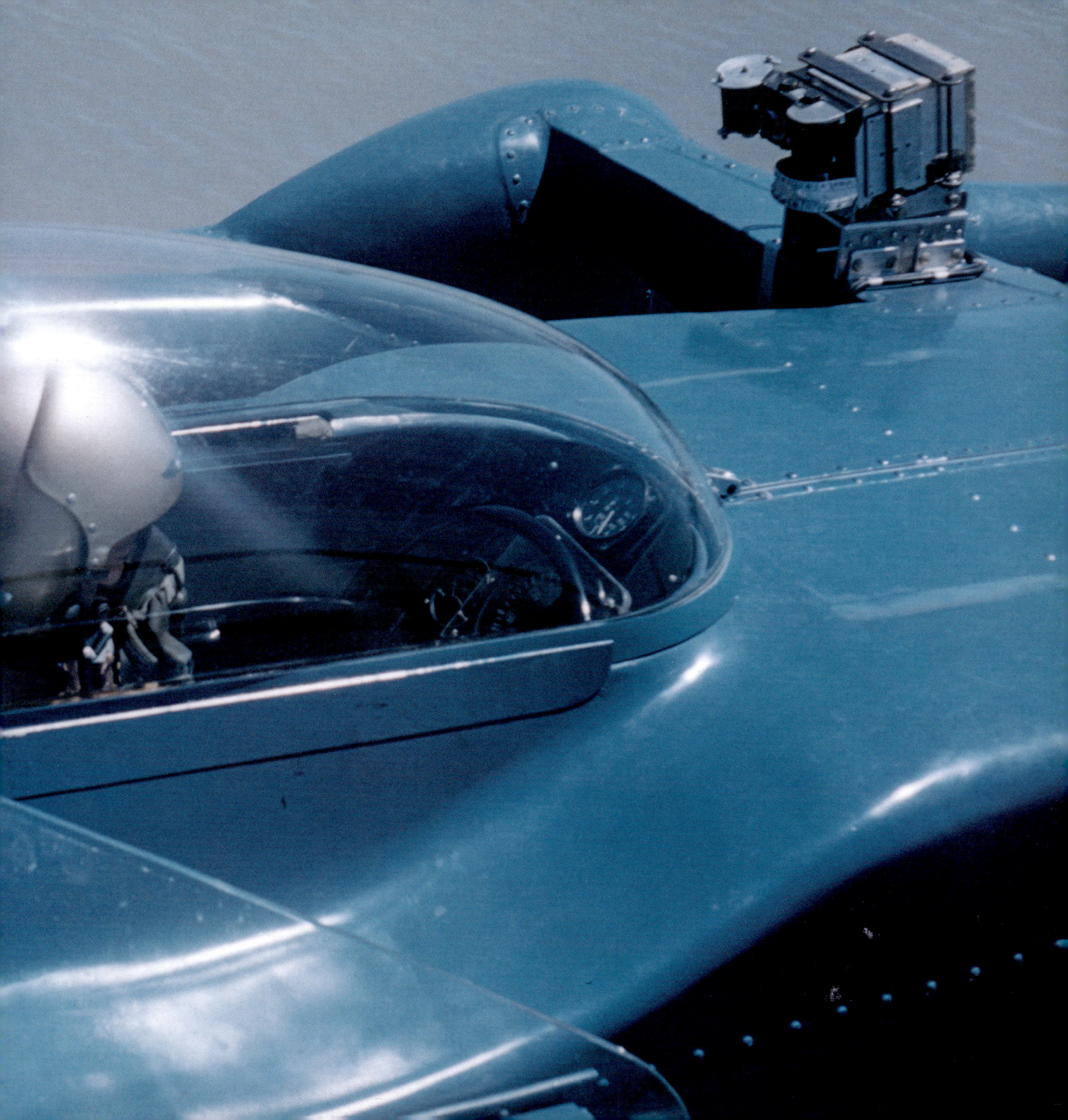

Report 4 from Canandaigua, 30th July 1957

Drastic steps have been taken for improving lake control conditions. Improvements include additional patrol vessels and laying some 10 miles of yellow, air-filled, plastic tubing, about 100 feet offshore on both banks about 1.5 hours prior to trials. This forms a road enclosing the course and marks an area which no pleasure boats should enter.

Mrs Samuels and family with John Fenn, Donald and his Rolleiflex.

Report 5 from Canandaigua 1st August 1957

First safety trial with Bluebird on the water on 4th July; weather and lake conditions are against the team with strong winds of 30 to 40 mph. Interest in Bluebird Park is high with good attendance. Time spent preparing the slip and drilling the patrol boats property. The Bluebird team is ready for serious trials. BB will be standing by from Wednesday 31st July to Saturday 3rd August, for a timed run.

But the right conditions never came and Donald anxious to win the Butlin Award before the end of the year and get back to England to run on Coniston, made a snap decision to send myself, Andrew Brown and Jim Hinton back to prepare for the attempt while he stayed behind to arrange for the return of Bluebird.

Leo Villa

Photo by Donald of the sponsors and families, K7 team and Gina.

John Fenn, Jim Hinton, Leo, Maurie and the Skipper.

CONISTON 1957

By October we were at Coniston working in a temporary shed built by Mobil, who were still sponsoring Campbell/Bluebird. We were now staying at the Sun Hotel with Connie Robinson who had sold the Black Bull Pub and acquired the Sun Inn. Bluebird was also back at Coniston by mid-November; Maurie, Jeff Spencer and Jim Hinton of Dunlop's were working with me. She was given a thorough check and slipped into the water for an engine test. She started without difficulty, but as soon as I stepped up the revs the most unnatural noises came out of the engine. I shut her off and an examination revealed that the blade tips of the axial compressor had been badly damaged by something solid which had been sucked into the air intake. For the three days the lake surface had been perfect, so I got the team together and asked them if they were prepared to go on a bander, what we called an all-night session, and to have the boat ready for Donald tomorrow when he arrived. They agreed.

Connie with Uncle Ken in the cocktail bar at the Sun.

When we took the engine out, we discovered that several rivets from the rear end of the engine intake had been sucked into the compressor. The rivets were replaced, the area reinforced, and the spare engine installed. By 5 a.m. the next morning, the peaceful atmosphere of Ruskin's favourite beauty spot was shattered by the whine of the spare Beryl and Bluebird was again ready to go! The weather held up and by Tuesday 7th November Donald made three runs; north–south at 188.00 mph, south–north at 243.41 mph, north–south at 253.84 mph. The code for this year was "Scrub!" which indicated a new record for Donald of 239.07 mph and the Butlin Trophy for the second year in succession. Meanwhile the plans for the 600 mph Bluebird motor car were coming along nicely.

Leo Villa

CONISTON 1958

One day Donald called on Joan and me and introduced us to an attractive young cabaret star from Belgium whom he had recently met. Her name was Tonia Bern, and I could see that she was something special and I wasn't altogether surprised when he invited Joan and me to be present at their wedding on 24th December 1958.

This time in October we set up shop in a new boatshed built for us by BP. On the early trial runs Donald was still unhappy at speeds over 260 mph. To increase directional stability, the Norris brothers had designed a steel fin, and this was now quickly made by Vickers. This fin was to be attached centrally under the transom, and it projected about 4 inches below the rear planing shoe. It was wedge-sectioned and razor sharp along the leading edge.

By 10th November conditions were ideal and Donald went out and raised his record to 248.62, still under his 250 mph target, but high enough to gain him another Butlin Trophy and the award. Donald reported when he came in that he now had a lot more confidence in the Bluebird and felt that, given the right conditions, he could now take her up to 300 mph.

Leo Villa

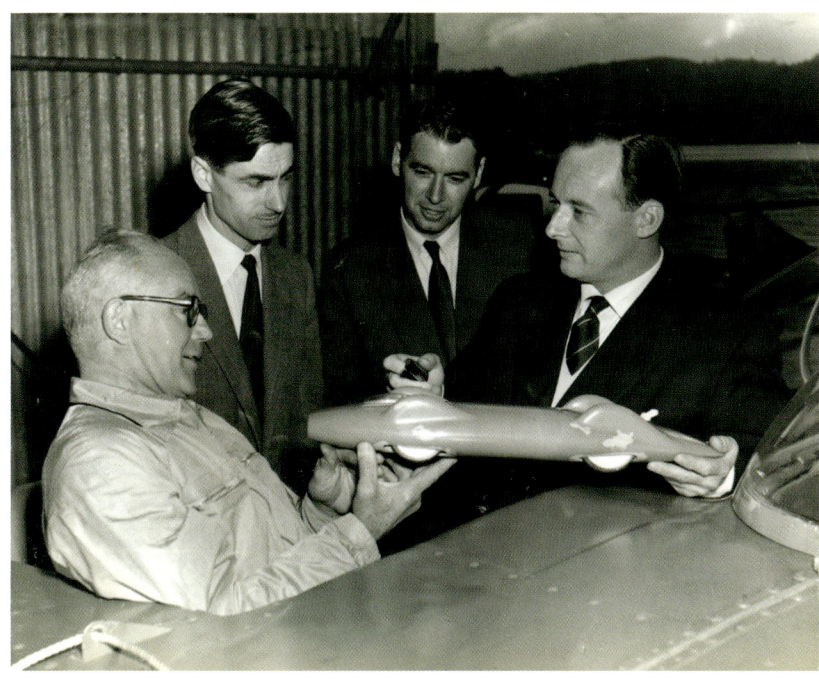

Although the plans for the new Bluebird motor car were now beginning to crystallise, I saw very little of Donald at that stage as I had my hands full with some further modifications which we planned to make to the Bluebird boat. The biggest alteration was the fitting of a tail fin to accommodate a parachute and for additional directional stability. Donald had been worried about the length of the run available to him at Coniston, and for some time past we had talked about experimenting with a parachute. We were also raising the height of the fairings covering the top side of the forward planing shoes. This, apart from giving the boat a better appearance, was calculated to decrease the tendency of the nose to lift at speed, still our biggest bugbear. On this record attempt we were being backed by BP and I saw relatively little of Donald, as he was busy whipping up support for the CN7 car project with the Norris brothers, who had built three wind tunnel models with different streamlined configurations. By the time we were ready to leave for Coniston, they had decided on a final shape for the Bluebird car. They brought the model up to Coniston during the attempt.

FANCY FREE 1956-58

JOHN FENN

Alan Crompton had had a serious accident and had taken up water skiing as therapy. In 1956 he approached John Fenn of Fenn & Wood Ltd, builders of high-speed sports boats since the war and very popular amongst the advocates of the newly developing sport of water skiing. Alan wanted to set up a challenge to water ski non-stop Dover–Calais–Dover and asked John to assist him; as this had never been done, as a promotional project for Fenn & Wood, it was excellent. Alan also wondered about the possibilities of getting Donald Campbell to drive one of Fenn & Wood's Meteor speedboats. Donald Campbell was contacted and the project outlined to him and as he was rather starved of media exposure, he was delighted to assist. In 1956 there was not the same amount of traffic in the Channel as today. Alan stood well on his skis there and back for the non-stop event and there were looks of astonishment as they entered Calais harbour at high speed, circled it, cut a few fishing lines and departed in great haste.

John and Heather Fenn with the Meteor's driver.

EUROPEAN TOUR

In 1958 John Fenn decided to enter the Le Bourget 24-hour speedboat race held at Aix-les-Bains on Lac Le Bourget in La Belle France. Having accompanied Donald to Canandaigua, John had become a member of the Bluebird team and it was decided that it would be a great opportunity for Bluebird to do a few demo runs and if conditions were OK, to go for the record during speed week. Bluebird travelled by road via the Brussels Exhibition and Paris, as always, causing rather a stir en route. 200,000 people crowded around Le Bourget, coming from all over the Rhone-Alpes region with a caravan of 10,000 cars. During his high-speed trials Donald reached 360 km/h (225 mph).

Hier 15,000 Parisiens ont admiré L'Oiseau Bleu du Recordman Anglais, Monsieur Donald Campbell, sur La Place des Invalides.

This afternoon, Donald Campbell will rejoin his Oiseau Bleu which is at present on display at the Esplanade des Invalides before continuing its journey to Aix-les-Bains: The convoy transporting L'Oiseau Bleu left Brussels on Saturday, at 1600 Hours where it had been on show in the British Pavilion of the Exhibition and arrived here in Paris at two o'clock in the morning. It will remain opposite the Dome des Invalides until tomorrow morning at six o'clock, when it will resume its journey to Chalon en route to Aix-les-Bains. Two engineers (of our acquaintance) are guarding the Bluebird.

Le Dauphiné Libéré, 23 Juin, 1958

CONISTON 1959

April, back at Coniston again and the team now included my nephew Phil Villa, son of my brother who works at the Savoy. Maurie and Brian also came to Coniston with us, and we were soon accompanied by Commander Greville Howard and Peter Barker, a friend of Donald's who had come up to handle press relations. By 14th May we were all standing by. The lake seemed calm and placid but I held Donald back because a slight movement of my own boat indicated a swell which was not visible on the surface of the water. As soon as it settled down I gave him the OK but warned him to feel his way. Within a few minutes he was flashing past, going at a cracking pace, rock steady, and her trim perfect. At the south end, Donald requested his speed. It was 275 mph precisely. As soon as the wash had died away, I gave him the all clear for the return run which he covered at 245.55 mph, an average for the two runs of 260.33 mph: another new record, another Butlin Trophy, his fourth ... plus the knowledge that he had at last put the record above the 250-mph mark. Tonia was at the pier head to greet him, looking pale and worried. This was our easiest record to date. The weather had been good, and there were no mechanical setbacks. We did hear, on the eve of the record run, that America was building a jet-boat to go after Donald's record.

Leo Villa

117

TONIA BERN-CAMPBELL

I first met Donald in 1958 at a publicity party given for me for my opening at the Savoy Hotel in London by Loraine Desmond in her apartment at Nell Gwynne House in Dolphin Square. Later Donald told me that he had bumped into a journalist that was coming to interview me and had asked him where he was going. 'I am going to interview Tonia Bern; she just arrived from Paris this morning.' 'Ah!' Donald said jokingly, 'I just saw her picture in the newspaper this morning, I wouldn't mind interviewing her myself.' 'Well come along Donald, it's an open party.'

Donald came into the room and I saw those incredible blue eyes and that charisma he had and I thought I've seen this man before – maybe he had interviewed me? He walked up to me; what he told me later was that he had seen me standing next to Loraine Desmond; we were both in tights with mini-skirts with very loose sweaters, it was winter, and he had thought to himself, well the two of them will do for me. He walked up to me and heard my accent and spoke French to me. I did not understand a word he said. I replied 'Monsieur, maybe you speak English, I understand you, yes?' and he put on that little boy face, as if he was being punished, a face that I would get to know very, very well, and I would melt each time and I said, 'I'm sorry, I am being naughty, actually your French is quite good.' 'No,' he said, 'I speak French like a Spanish cow' – Comme une vache Espagnole.

Suddenly everybody in the room disappeared and there was just the two of us: there was that link, like we were one, at once. 'Well,' he said, 'if you were not so busy I would take you out to dinner!' 'Oh!' I said, 'I am not busy' ... So he had to go and cancel with a girlfriend and I had to tell Loraine to call a boyfriend of mine that I was not going to his dinner party. Donald took me to Rules in Covent Garden, and ordered everything I disliked. He ordered brains and he ordered red wine, I did not drink wine in those days. That was it, that really was it; when we left Rules a couple of hours later Donald asked me which night club I wanted to go to and I said, '*No*, I want to go home with you.' 'What you mean I don't have to send you roses and start to court you?' 'No,' I said, 'it is a waste of time. Send them afterwards.' Three days later he proposed and I refused because I was not the marrying type, and I wanted a career, that was all I lived for, but he would not take no for an answer and said, 'I want to marry you.' I told him I can't cook, I like animals, but I don't like kids and I am a very unfaithful person, I would be a rotten wife. 'Well,' he said, 'I married two who promised to be good wives, so I'd like to try a rotten one for a change.' We got married three weeks from the day we met on Christmas Eve. He just swept me off my feet and suddenly showbusiness was not important any more, anything without him lost its importance.

Within a year of our marriage Donald made another attempt on the water speed record in 1959. I didn't like Coniston very much and the people there didn't like me either: they thought I was very showbiz, which I was.

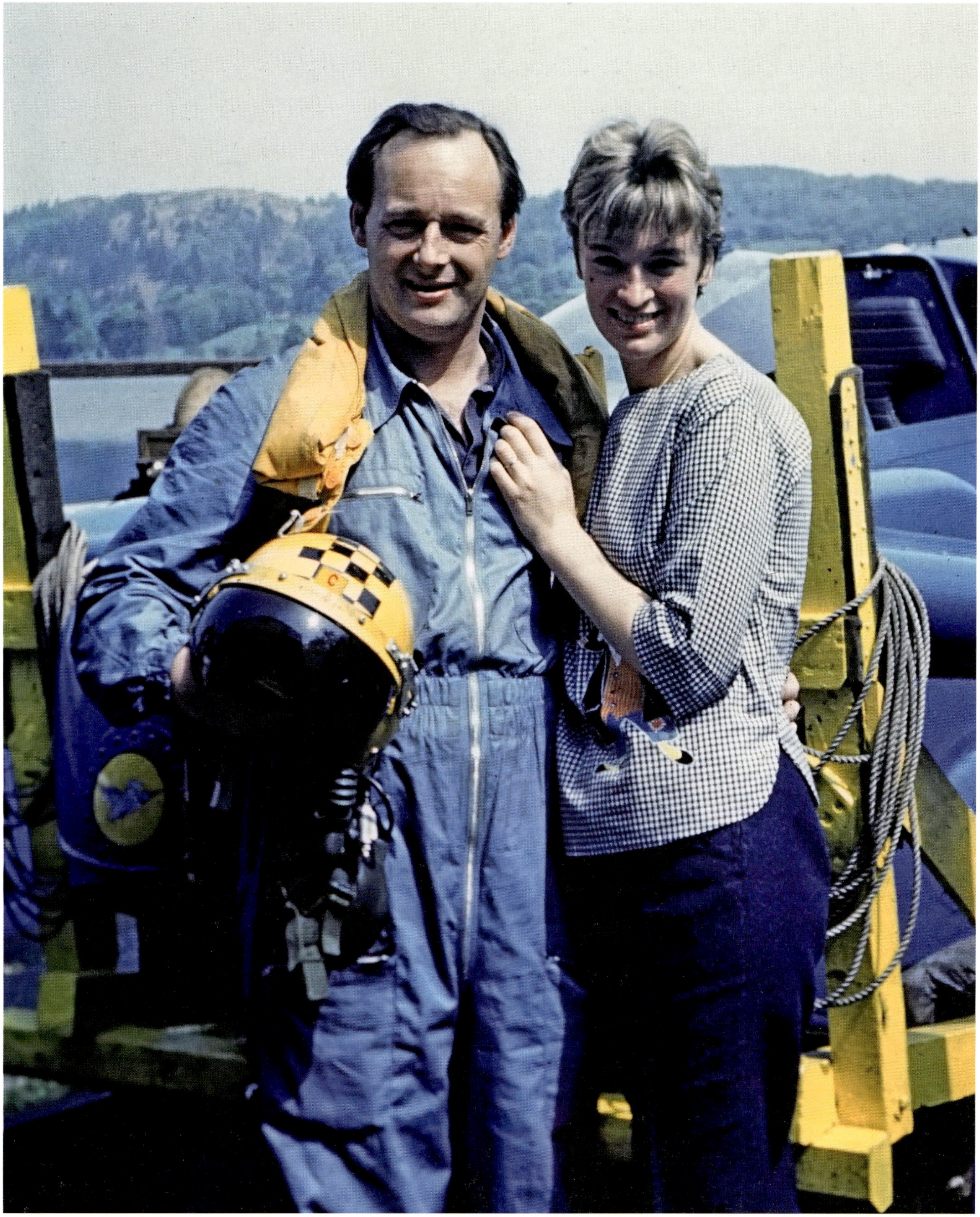

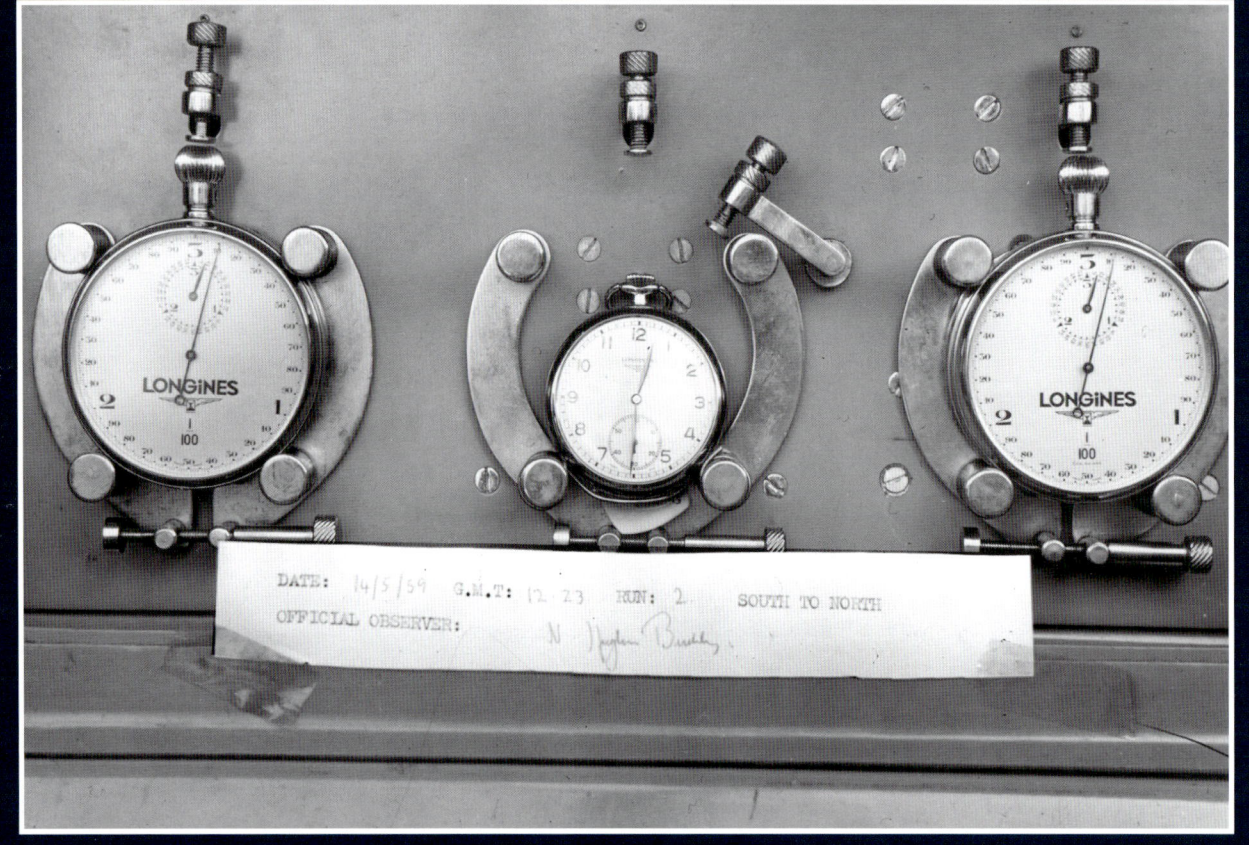

Longines North timings at Coniston with the Chronocinégines set up on the platform. The white post that is the finishing line is still visible today just below the water's surface.

John Fenn (centre) with the Official Observer Norman Buckley (seated).

Donald with the Chronocinégines at the Longines factory in St. Imier in August, 1966, having gained the company's support for the final attempt.

How Long a Mile
1960–1963

BLUEBIRD WORLD LAND SPEED RECORD ATTEMPT

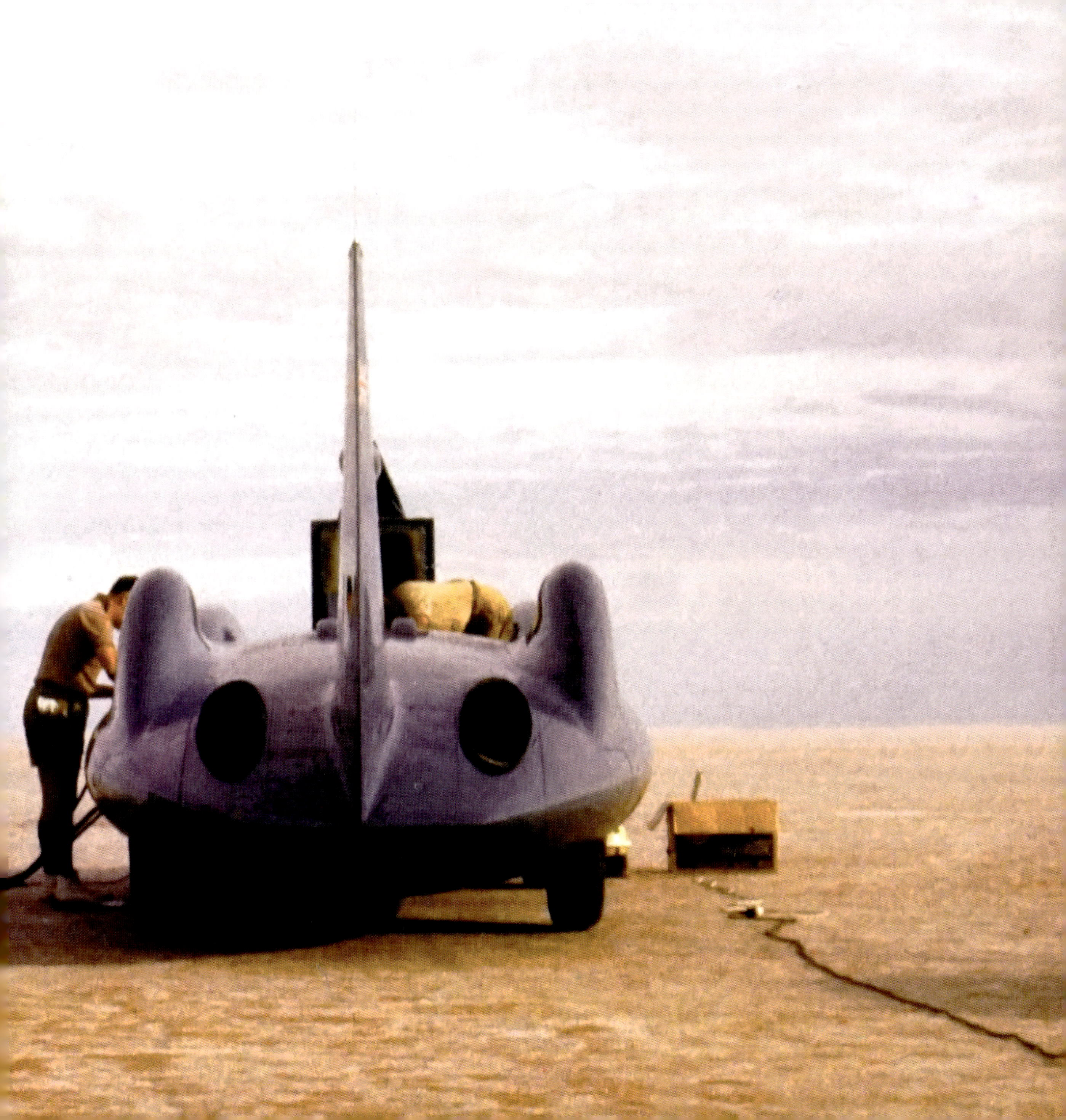

Campbell-Norris 7

The first step in getting support for a project of this kind is to start the publicity going, and once word got around that Donald was going after 400+mph on land, he felt certain that support would be forthcoming. After all, he had now proved himself on both sides of the Atlantic.

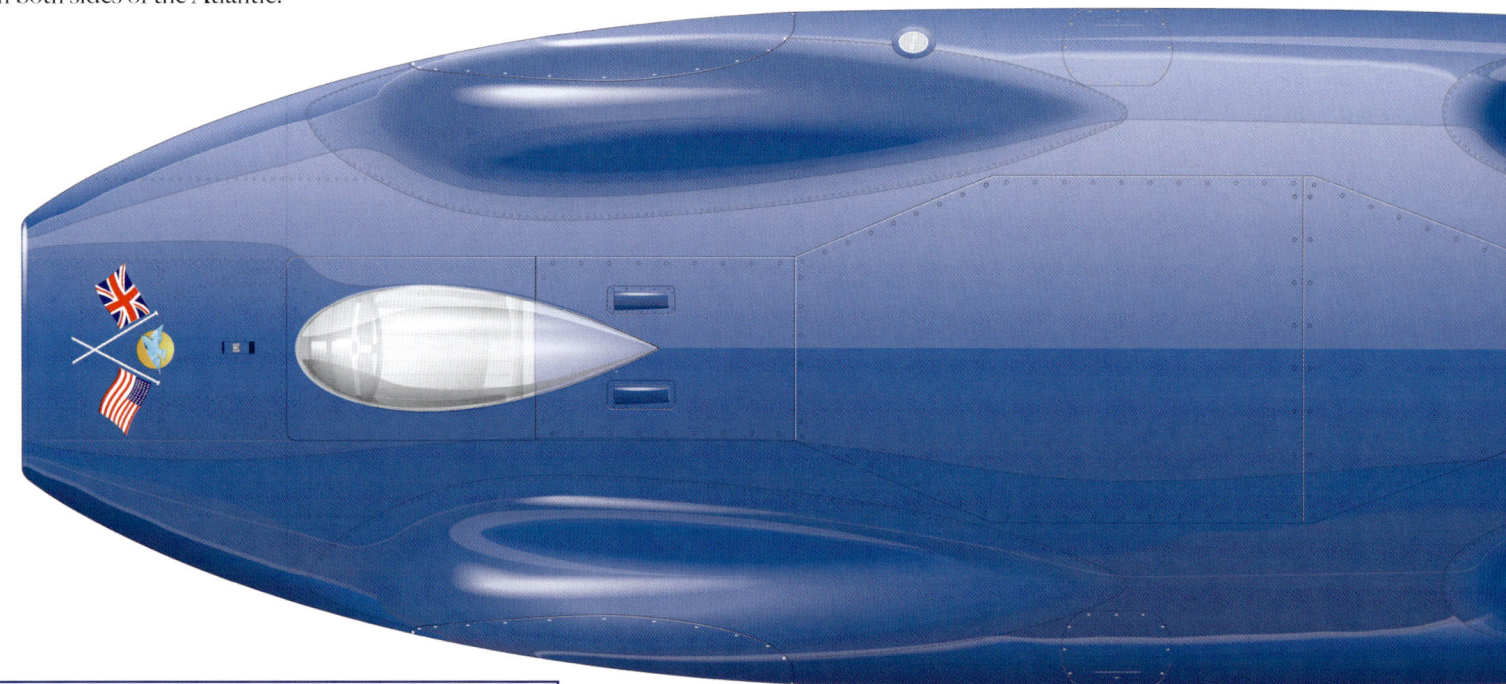

Campbell-Norris-Bluebird, Project 7	
Length	30 feet
Width	8 feet
Height (without fin)	4 feet 9 inches
Wheelbase	13 feet 6 inches
Track	5 feet 6 inches
All-up weight	4 tons
Power unit	Proteus 705
Tyres	Dunlop interwoven web ply 4 52 inches diameter × 8.52 inches section
Brakes	Girling discs, parachute and air brakes
Fuel	BP Avtur, 25-gallon capacity tank

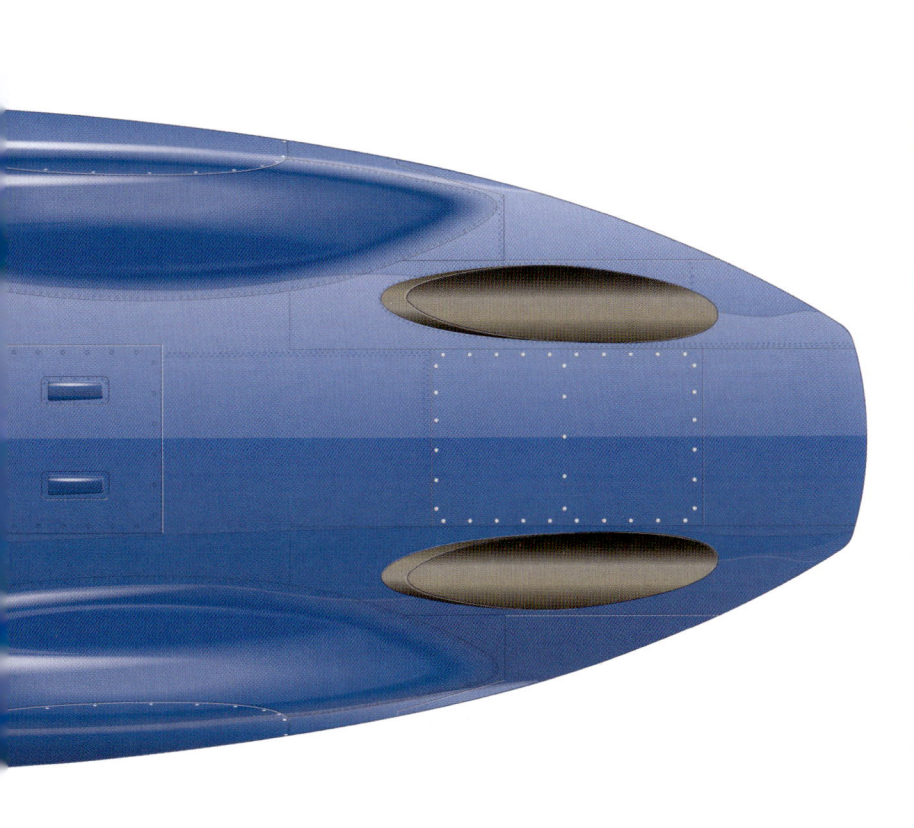

Designers

The Norris brothers approached their part of the problem from the other end: firstly, what speed did he want to attempt? Second, what engines were available that would be capable of giving that speed? Third, could they get tyres and wheels built capable of standing up to the proposed speeds? Finally, there was the question of who was going to build the car. The body, various components like the axles, gearbox, and steering gear would, of course, be built and supplied by the various firms specialising in these parts. In the initial stages all that Donald could do was put out feelers to see whether the various firms like Joseph Lucas and David Brown were likely to be interested once he got the project off the ground. It was quite clear, even during the initial discussions, that this was going to be the biggest record-breaking venture of all time, probably the biggest project of its kind handled by one man.

One man band

The organisation of support on this scale was in itself a tremendous piece of administration. Indeed, most men would have regarded it as a full-time job, but Donald managed to combine it with record-breaking, and between this time, when the project was first discussed with the Norris brothers, and 1960, when the car was finally built, Donald broke his own World Water Speed Record four times. Donald continued his record-breaking activities for two reasons: he had to keep himself in the public eye while the car was being planned and constructed, and indeed, the amount of sponsorship he could expect would very largely depend on the success of his interim record attempts and the sort of press that they got. The other reason Donald had to continue breaking records was that it offered him a source of revenue.

Leo Villa

The Boys

I became involved with the installation of the motor and the gearboxes into the Bluebird at Motor Panels in Hollingbrook Lane, Coventry. They were building one-off bodies for people like Leyland trucks and, towards the time that we were there, they'd dropped down to making stainless steel sinks. Their stock-in-trade really was body design work and at Motor Panels there must have been from six to eight people, the old-time panel beaters, all the big wheel fairings were done on what they call a rolling machine and they were all hand rolled and hand-fitted. Leo was constantly running round like a blue-arsed fly and by the time I got there the body was ready to take the engine. I wanted to make sure that we could line the Proteus up and dropped it in after Leo sorted out the gearboxes and then we lifted the engine back out again.

Ray Govier – Bristol-Siddeley Proteus technician

Design team: Lew, Don Stevens, Ken, Fred Wooding and Jerzy Orlowski.

John Stollery, Leo, G.E. Cook, Cliff Polley, Peter Church, Ken Norris, Dennis Burgess and Maurie Parfitt.

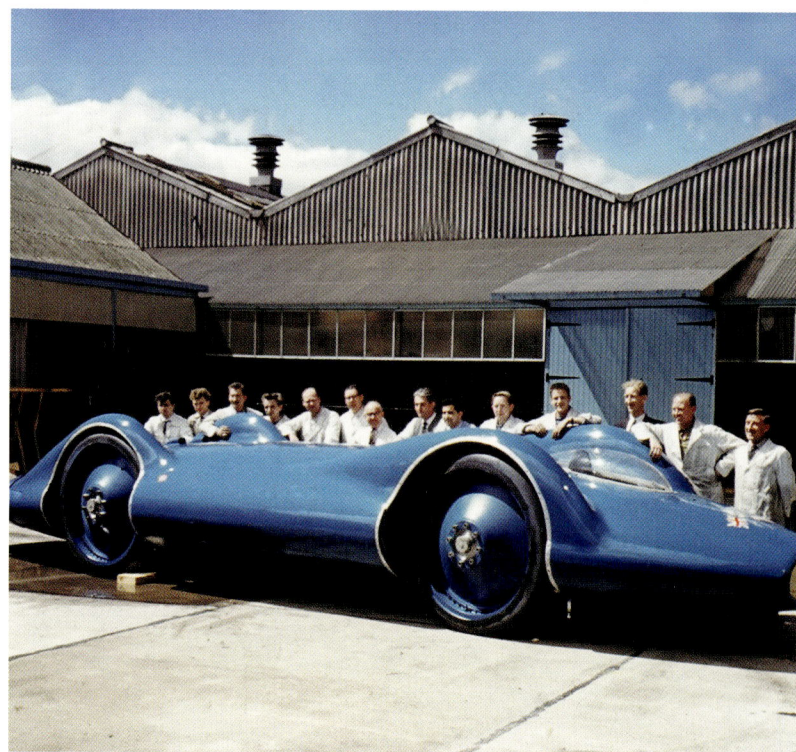

Goodwood

CN7 was completed by May 1960 and two months later we were on the Goodwood Motor Circuit for a press preview and a trial run. Donald took her round the course with the brakes on; the idling speed on the Bluebird with no throttle at all was around 80 mph. The press took a lot of pictures and Donald did a lot of talking. It was now just a question of going out to Utah, doing a couple of high-speed runs and coming back with the land speed record under our belt. That was all that was supposed to be involved. Little did we know!

Leo Villa

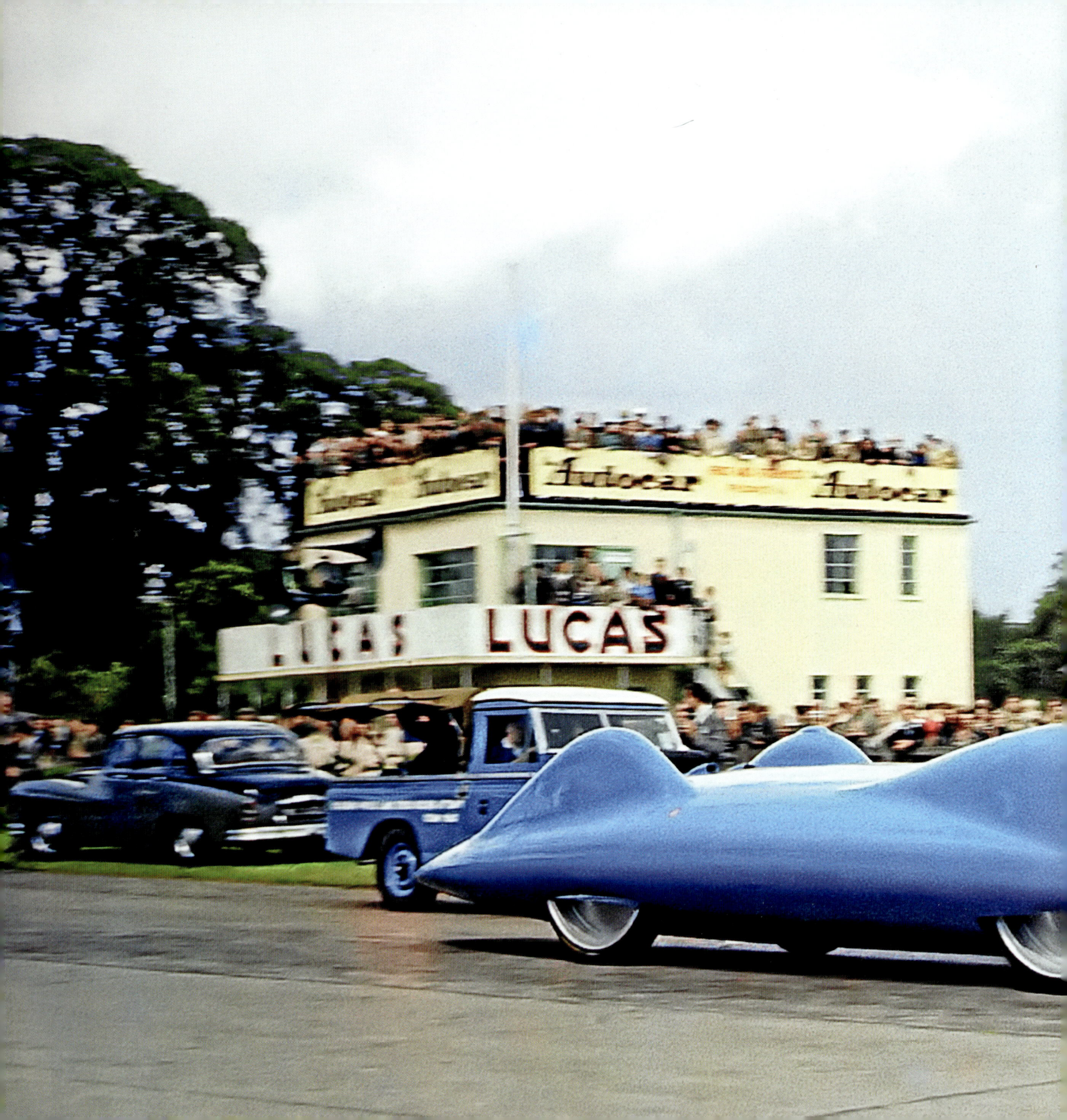

Autocar
Autocar
LUCAS
LUCAS

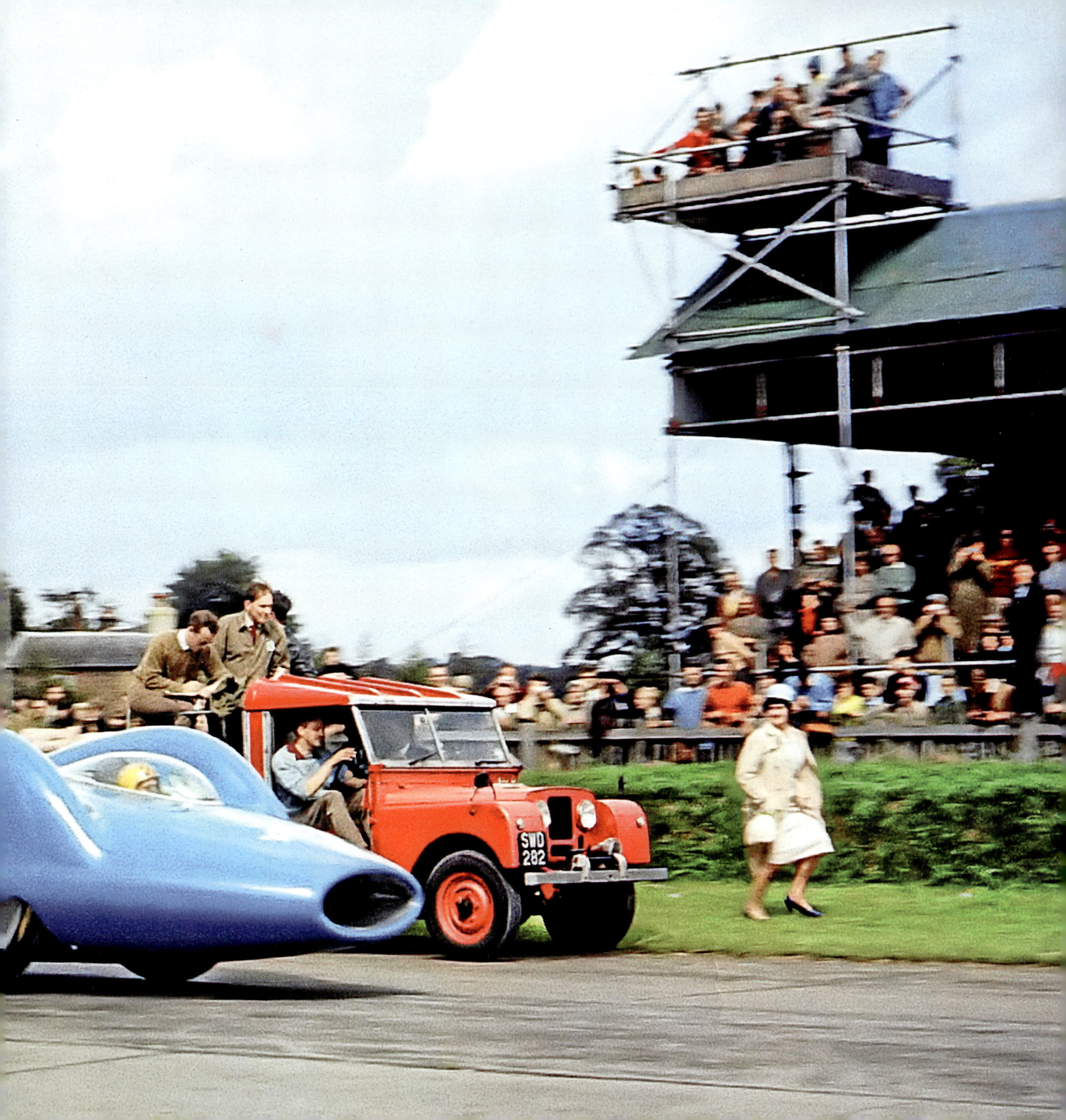
SWD
282

Utah 1960

Leo

The salt was in an appalling condition it had changed completely since our last visit in 1935 with the Old Man. It was a mushy substance: blackish, humid and treacherous. The flats occupied a vast area of hundreds of square miles, but the actual course was short, only about 11 miles and to beat the record we knew that Bluebird would have to reach a speed of at least 300 mph inside the first mile and a half of the run. It had cost a small fortune to take Bluebird to Bonneville and the attempt was surrounded by a blaze of publicity, and when Donald asked me what we should do, I told him, 'Let's give it a try, but for God's sake Don take it easy old boy!'

The Skipper

We arrived in Salt Lake City and from that moment everything started to go wrong: Tonia fell ill upon arrival, there was dissension in the base camp at Wendover and, worse still, Leo was very preoccupied with the condition of the salt track. Out on the lake Leo said, 'Skipper we shouldn't run: the salt has completely changed since we were last here with the Old Man.' He was right, then, it was glaring white and hard and as I looked down at the salt, my mind went back 25 years when as a schoolboy I had watched my father become the first man to do 300 mph on land. We walked down the track. Leo was right, it was horrible.

Tonia:
Mon homme

It was when Donald took the car to Utah that he started to involve me in his attempts. He never really wanted me to go with him because he was always frightened that something would happen and I would have to watch it, he really didn't think it was the place for a woman, but I told him that as I had given up my career, he had to let me have his fully, 100%, and in the end he agreed on the condition that a girlfriend would accompany me. Vera Freeman came to Bonneville. It was after that bid that he made me an official member of the team and I was given the nickname Fred.

The flats

Donald's first land speed record was very exciting for him, extremely exciting for him, because he'd done the water speed record and I think he got a little bit bored with it, because every time having broken his own record so easily, so when we got to Utah he was looking forward to it. He met Craig Breedlove and they immediately befriended each other and decided they would break each other's records and make it exciting for the world. We all thought it was a great idea. After Donald's first run in the car, he came back and told me that it was much easier than on water, much easier. The problem with the crash was, as it was a turbine-driven car, a car driven by all four wheels, he accelerated too hard.

We designed that car for 600 mph.
We had gears for 400 and gears
for 600 mph. He had the gears for
400 in it, at the time of the crash.

Lew Norris

Little old Speed King

It was the first run that Donald really wanted to accelerate the car and put his foot down. We were travelling up behind with Leo in another car and, lo and behold, we caught a flash of blue out of the top of the dust cloud and we realised it was the car – it was airborne! So we added about another ton to the 100 we were doing already and shot off to look for it. Bluebird was a quarter of a mile off-track and on the way had lost its wheels and suspension. Luckily it had slewed and stayed upright, and we could see Donald's head wobbling around, so we knew he hadn't been killed. When we got up to the car, the engine was purring away, lovely; we went onto the top and yanked up the emergency release on the canopy, and it all looked perfect: the whole structure had contained Donald. From the tracks it looked like he had lost all four wheels, the torque had been too high, and maybe he put his foot down a little too heavily, getting used to a turbine engine; you don't get a response immediately, it idles for a moment and you put your foot down further and then of course it hits you up the backside and off you go. My records show he was doing about 370 when he went off; it slued, went into wind, went up like a wing, rolled over and came down and bounced just off track. The G-meter registered over 6G during the gyrations.

Ken Norris

Screeching

Three green numerals were imprinted in my mind: 365 mph — 0.7G acceleration, 100% power. Then it was dark and out of the darkness came a bang to the left side of my head followed by a sledge hammer blow to the right. I had no idea where I was or why, only that I existed. It was dark, very dark. A shattering, screeching, pain-racked, pitch-black Hell. I wished it would stop and that I knew where I was and what I was doing. Then it dawned on me: I was in the cockpit of Bluebird in rough salt and that there had been an accident.

News of the World, 1964

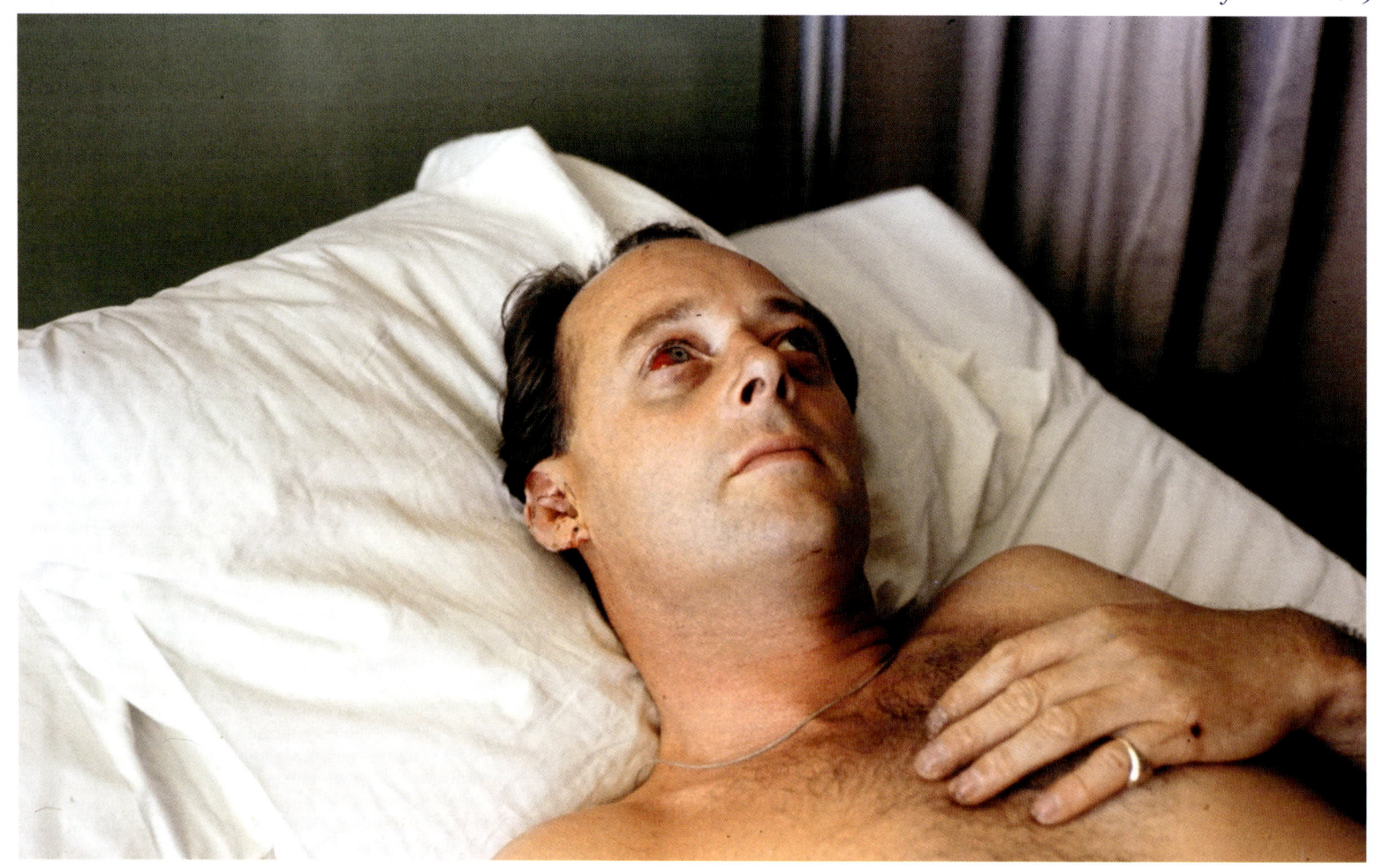

We were following in another car and finally we reached the crash, and they were lifting him out of the car all covered in blood, but he was moving his head like somebody trying to wake up. He told Peter Carr, our project manager, 'Don't let her see me. Don't let her come in the ambulance,' because he did not know how badly he was injured, or if he was dying, and he didn't want me to see that he was still worried. Peter pushed me into the passenger seat in the front of the ambulance and then we'd been driving about 20 minutes and there was a little knock on the window between the driver and the back of the ambulance and it was Peter Carr. He said, 'Skipper says that the family jewels are OK,' and I knew he was OK.

He had three broken ribs, a fractured skull, a contusion of the brain and he had lost some cerebral fluid which was trickling out of an ear, so we could not fly. After he was discharged from the hospital we did not think that there was anything else wrong with him. We had a friend, Ray Ryan, who owned the El Mirador Hotel in Palm Springs and it was whilst we were staying there in Beverly Hills that Donald started having cold sweats and suddenly he would feel very frightened. So he went to see a neurologist, who said that there was nothing that could be done for this condition: 'You are suffering from what fighter pilots got during the war: your adrenaline starts running for no reason at all ... All I can give you is some sleeping pills so you don't get them at night.' It was awful.

Tonia

Playing-a-round

Whilst we were in Palm Springs Donald met Clark Gable, William Holden, Henry Fonda, James Garner, all the stars of the time, and they played golf together. In fact, he played with President Dwight Eisenhower, who was President at the time, and he was very curious about the crash and wanted to see all the photographs of Bluebird. Donald showed him the crash photos and Eisenhower looked at me and asked, 'How does she feel about it?' Donald replied, 'She's a pillar of strength.' 'Well, honey I tell you a thing: if I had to be involved with anything like that, I'd rather be in the cockpit than watch it from the side-lines.'

Donald discussed his neurological problem with the President, which he had a lot then; he would suddenly stop playing golf, he'd be frightened for no reason, and Eisenhower told him the same thing as the neurologist, that it was a shock reaction that fighter pilots suffered during the war: don't worry, it will eventually go away. But Donald went through a whole year of hell, absolute hell, and eventually we returned to England.

Rodeo Drive, Hollywood.

He had always wanted to be a pilot, so I told him that as long as he had these adrenaline problems he wouldn't be able to make another record attempt: 'So why don't you take your pilot's licence; at least you will be doing something useful: you've always wanted to do it.' 'That's a bloody good idea Bobo.' By 1962 he felt himself getting better, then he had to do his first solo flight, whilst he was up there he had an attack and when he came back he told me; I was up there in the clouds and suddenly I got so scared, I got the cold sweats and I started shaking, I thought to myself if I don't pull myself together I'll crash and die. Suddenly the problem went ... and from then on he was fine!

Of course right after the car crashed, when Donald was still in hospital, we had received a wire from Sir Alfred Owen saying that everybody was ready to rebuild Bluebird which was an amazing thing. Donald cried, he absolutely cried, when he got the telegram; he said, 'They had every right not to believe in me.'

Telegram in reply from Palm Springs, California to Alfred Owen, 26/10/60:

Deeply regret unable to be with you tonight: in terms of human feeling: your message of confidence and continued support received whilst in hospital meant much: and is profoundly appreciated. Bluebird was outstanding in every way: my confidence completely unshaken in this superb machine: that I survived this incredible crash is tremendous tribute to all concerned with the design and construction: with renewed thanks for your kind message and all you have so generously done to further this great British enterprise:

Kindest Regards:
Donald Campbell

Ray Ryan outside the Beverly Hills Hilton.

Crash re-design 1963

After the Bonneville crash Bluebird was rebuilt for the 1963 Lake Eyre attempt. Exterior changes included the replacement of the Perspex canopy with a stronger fibre-glass version with a tiny port-hole and a small flat square windscreen. The engine was upgraded to 755 with 5,000 hp. A new Hussenot telemetry system was installed measuring pitch, roll, yaw, acceleration, power, speed and suspension movement.

The main visible change was the addition of an aerodynamic tail fin to the rear for extra stability, with removable sections to alter its size and shape during trials.

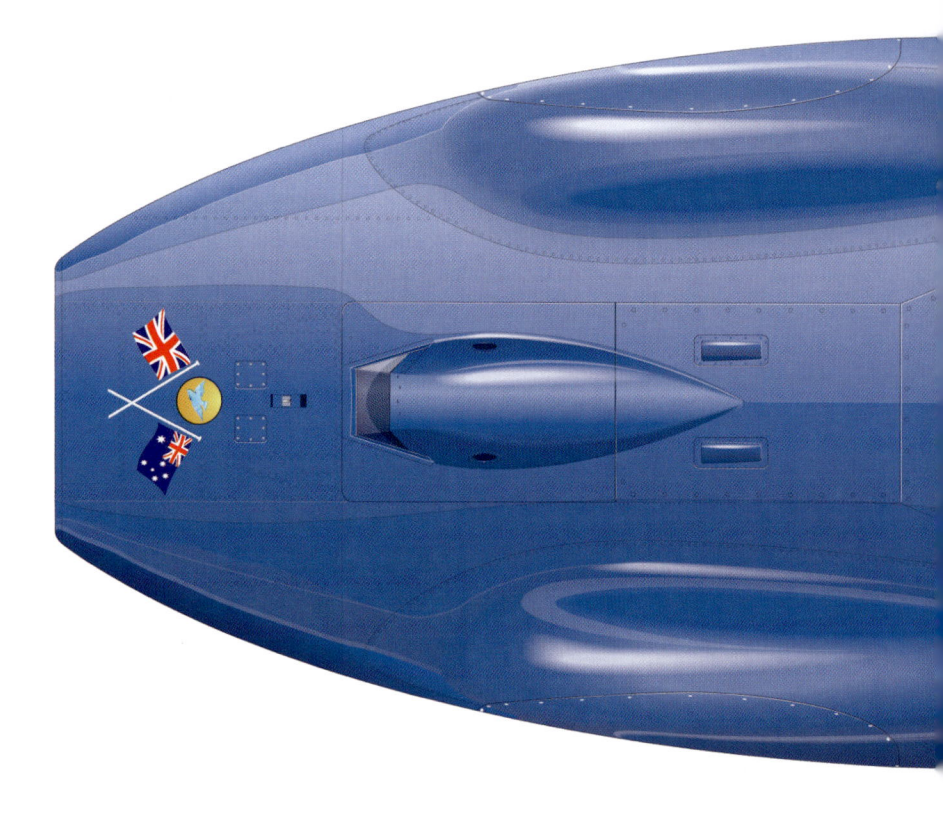

Campbell-Norris-Bluebird, Project 7 - 1963 re-design	
Length	30 feet
Width	8 feet
Height (with fin)	8 feet 9 inches
Wheelbase	13 feet 6 inches
Track	5 feet 6 inches
All-up weight	4 tons
Power unit	Proteus 755
Tyres	Dunlop interwoven web ply 4
	52 inches diameter × 8.52 inches section
Brakes	Girling discs, parachute and air brakes
Fuel	BP Avtur, 25-gallon capacity tank

137

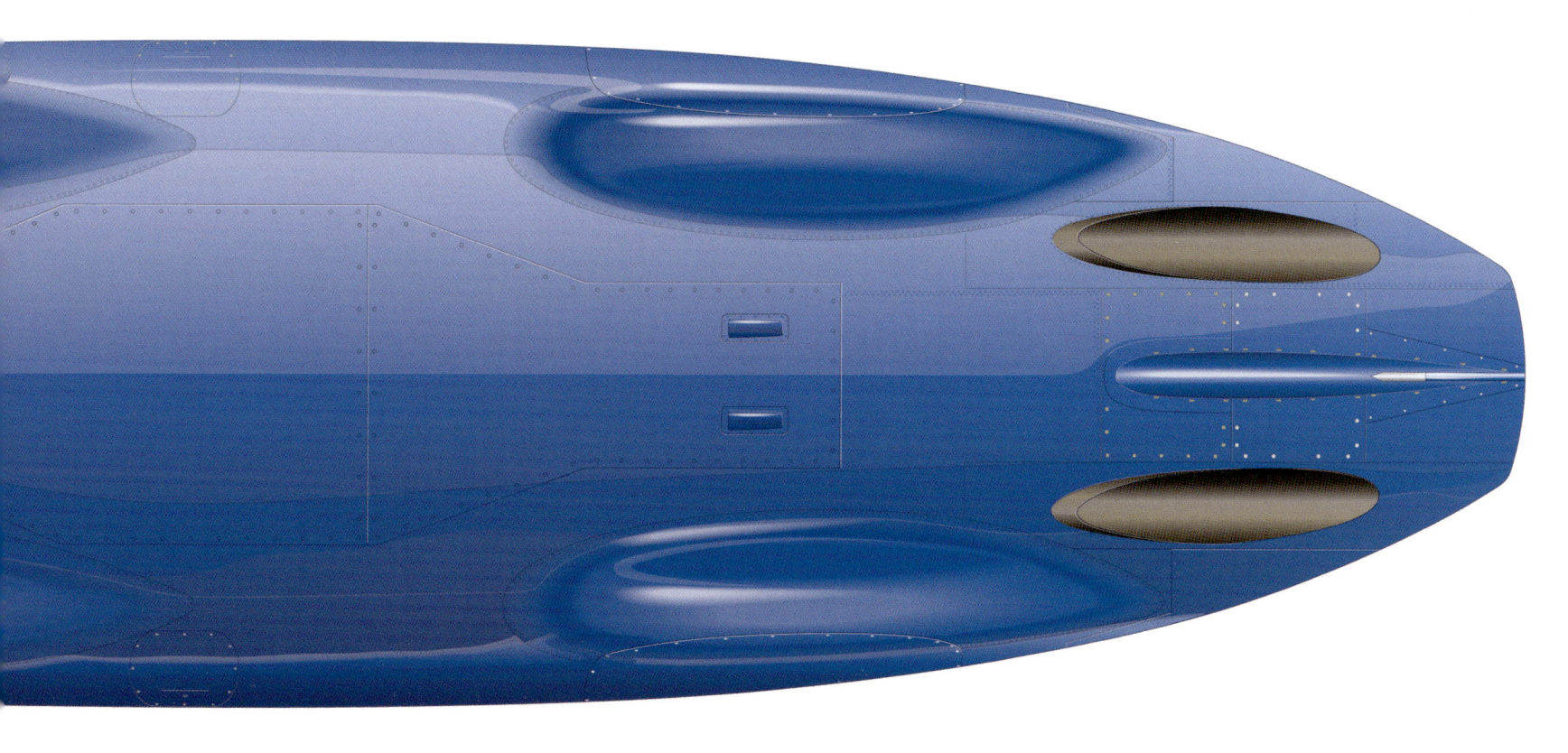

Lake Eyre 1963

The moment Donald recovered, his first aim was to find another salt track to run on. He did not want to go back to Utah and so with BP he started looking into going to Australia and eventually he found Muloorina in the outback, what a delightful place that turned out to be then we started the preparation; there was no doubt about me going with the team.

Tonia

The curse of Lake Eyre

Lake Eyre in South Australia offers 20 miles of hard, dry, level salt. Records showed major floods to be rare and irregular whilst surface water from local rain occurred only occasionally and was of a temporary nature. The average rainfall was half an inch per month. A lease of the area could ensure privacy so that a new machine could be worked up to record speeds gradually and progressively by a scientific predetermined plan, which called for a total of sixty-three runs. Track preparation commenced on schedule at the beginning of March 1963. 30 miles of access road and causeway, across bogs surrounding the vast area of hard salt at the centre of the lake, were completed to schedule on 15th March.

Conditions should have been ideal. 24 hours after completion of the causeway down onto the lake, intense rain began and continued for a week. The course area was flooded to a depth of 7 inches, or more than a full year's average rainfall. The entire programme was delayed; a track to run Bluebird, 15 miles long by 220 feet wide, had been fully graded. The first 9 miles, necessary for trials up to 300 mph, was machined clear of salt islands, fully marked and ready for use. Bluebird was in position on the track for the first trial at dawn the following day, but that night intense rain fell again. Spasmodically it continued over the next three weeks, finally causing major flooding and abandonment of the attempt. The photograph at the head of this page is, for me, the epitome of the bitter disappointment of the Lake Eyre expedition, disappointment fully shared by the many stalwart men who worked so hard to achieve our goal.

Donald Campbell BP report 345/654/dc/1963/09

Muloorina

Lake Eyre was surveyed in the middle of February. The surface was extremely hard and dry, but very rough. It was decided to establish the main base at the Muloorina homestead due to its facilities, even though it was 37 miles south of Bluebird's course area. Muloorina was a sheep station, founded, managed and owned by Eliot Price, our host.

Three tracks

Course preparation experiments began in February: test strips were laid down, and the most satisfactory results were obtained by using the graders working on the adjacent road and causeway. Initially three tracks were marked out with a light grading by 14-ton graders and early in March it was decided to use the most westerly run which was called the 'Bonython Run' in acknowledgment of the assistance given by Warren Bonython, whose exploration led to its selection in 1961. This course was chosen since it offered the most consistently dry area of the Madigan Gulf, with a potential length of 17 miles.

Grading and preparations

Course preparations were retarded, first by a 14-ton grader breaking through the salt crust at the northern end of the Bonython run and, secondly, by a 5-ton trailer loaded with salt through the centre of an island just milled at the ninth mile. The reduced surface-bearing strength was found to be due to softening of the salt crust by the preceding rains. The special Howard salt-milling machines, together with the Lundell elevating device, all functioned extremely well. Techniques for the removal of salt islands were developed and it became possible to remove one type of island to an accuracy of plus or minus an eighth of an inch. The process was necessarily slow. The entire area came under the control of the South Australian Police on 14th April and they were supported by units from the Army, the RAAF, equipped with a de Havilland, an Otter ambulance aircraft, the department of Civil Aviation and the GPO. An RAAF doctor was stationed at base camp during the entire operation.

On 17th March, after the Bonython Run had been graded over 15 miles, heavy local rail fell in the Lake Eyre region: Madigan Gulf was flooded to a depth of 7 inches. All equipment was removed from the lake surface to the causeway. The salt crust was found to be acting as a sponge, whilst the main water table rose by some 4 inches. The surface hardened sufficiently to permit preparations to start again on 5th April. This work proceeded concurrently with the marking of air-strips, service roads, photographic tower locations and the preparations of the facilities at Muloorina to accommodate 100 personnel.

Bluebird transit

On 10th February, CN7 with Bluebird K7 and associated equipment moved into the British Pavilion of the Melbourne International Trade Fair. The two machines comprised the principal British Government Exhibition. Bluebird was then moved from Melbourne to Adelaide by road in a convoy consisting of nine vehicles. Planned stops were made in major towns along the route, where schools were specially closed so that children could view the cavalcade. The car was exhibited in Adelaide and then transported to Muloorina by road and rail, arriving on 13th April.

The Bonython Run

The Bonython Run was prepared and marked out 9 miles in length by 220 feet. The first trial run was on 25th April. On the night of 24th-25th April rain fell again in the region and submerged large areas of the course, further rain threatened on the night of the 26th and the Bird was driven under power to the safety of the head of the causeway. Major rivers terminating in the Lake Eyre catchment were reported to be flowing through abnormally heavy rains and there were consequent floods in the Queensland and New South Wales areas. Numerous aerial searches were made, but it proved impossible to obtain any reliable information as to the river's rate of flow, or to make any accurate estimate as to the time they would take to reach our operational area in Madigan Gulf. The causeway was the one and only way off the salt lake and it continued to deteriorate through the rain fall. Key personnel were moved by air.

First speed trials

Bluebird behaved extremely well and mechanical adjustments were made with operations further delayed by spasmodic rain. On 4th May an emergency programme was put into force and maximum effort was concentrated on the Hobson's choice run, a course selected after intense aerial survey, since it was found possible to lay down a centre line completely free of salt islands. The overall length was 14 miles. It was necessary to compromise drastically on the course requirements laid down in 1961. Track preparation reverted to the method used for many years on the Bonneville salt flats, Utah, where a heavy joist was drawn slowly behind a tractor. This was possible due to the surface softening due to the rain.

She handles well

A number of highly satisfactory runs followed. Bluebird handled superbly well and inspired every confidence in all concerned. Speeds were gradually increased to a maximum of 260 mph. The final run was made on 13th May. Bluebird accelerated from rest to 175 miles per hour in 1 mile with 20% power, reaching a terminal velocity of approximately 260 at the third mile with the same power setting. Caution was necessary since areas of residual rain from the previous evening's fall covered the centre 6 miles of the course.

The Flying Doctor, Evan Green, Cliff Brebner of South Australia Police, Donald Campbell and Capt Dell.

'Bloody place. Filthy bloody place.' Donald Campbell.

Freaky storm

On 13th May a freak storm of violence unknown in winter months for the previous 36 years struck Lake Eyre. The course area was flooded to a depth of 2 inches and this was followed by an unexpected storm of even greater ferocity on the evening of 14th May. The water level rose rapidly and drastic action became necessary. At midnight Bluebird was driven under power through some 3 inches of water across the 5 miles from the base workshop to the safety of the causeway. The 32 miles of road from Muloorina to Sulphur Peninsula were turned into a quagmire and were passable only with the greatest difficulty, even to four-wheel-drive Land Rovers. The Bluebird was subsequently washed and inhibited at the head of the causeway then transported to Muloorina on a trailer towed by two military eight-wheel-drive recovery vehicles. The opportunity was taken to replace the brake discs and pads. On completion of this overhaul, which involved some three weeks' work, the vehicle was secured and stored in its packing case ready for 1964.

Disappointment

The operation, despite so many difficulties and disappointments, was characterised by a team spirit rarely achieved. This is to the greatest credit to all concerned and particularly when it must be appreciated that over 100 personnel were involved. Every indication showed the Proteus Bluebird to be fully capable of safely carrying the World Land Speed Record to substantially beyond 400 mph. Lake Eyre will clearly be unserviceable for a considerable time to come.

Louis Gossens, Donald's butler, with Leo and Maurie.

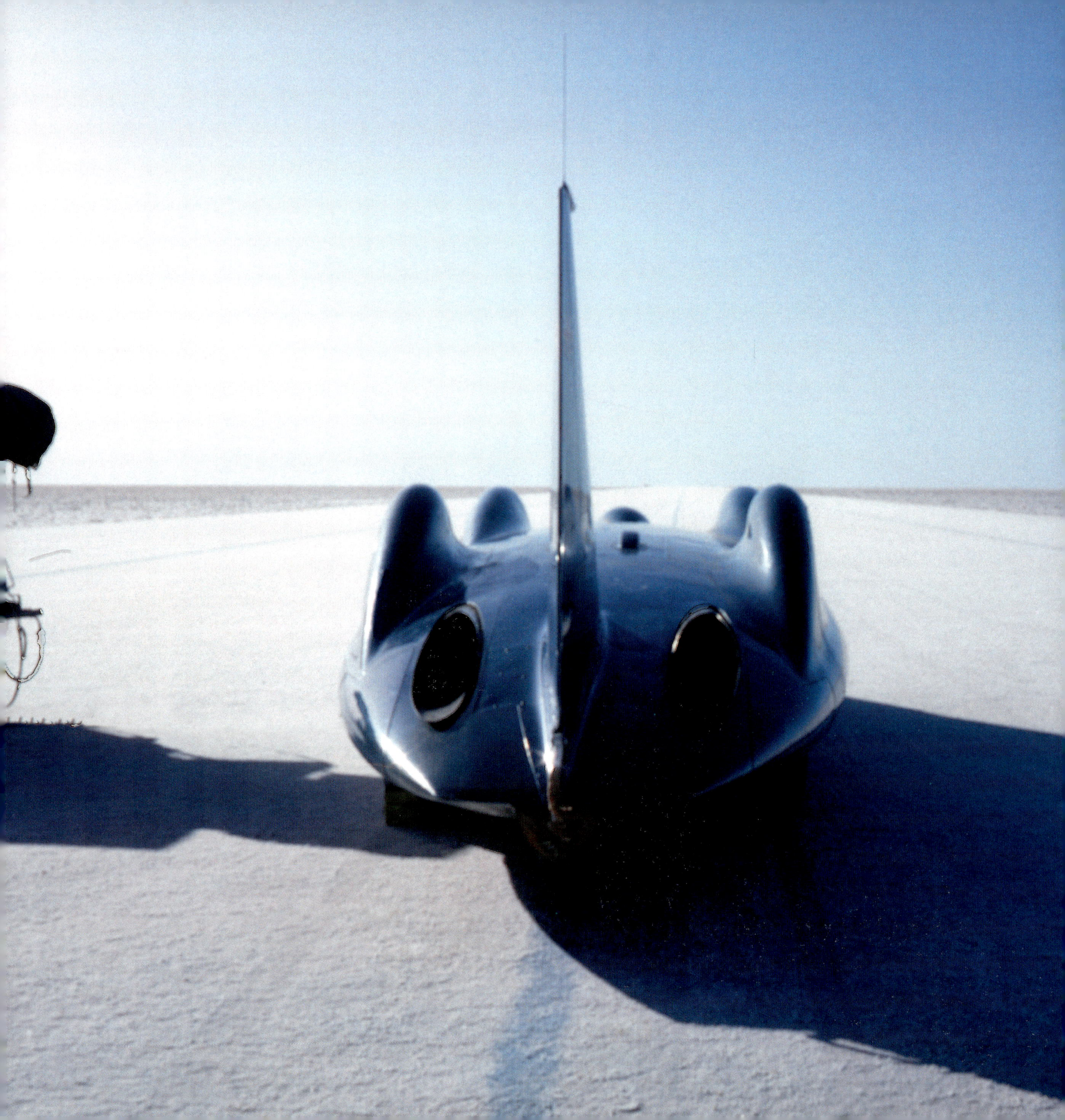

2-mile marker on Hobson's choice track.

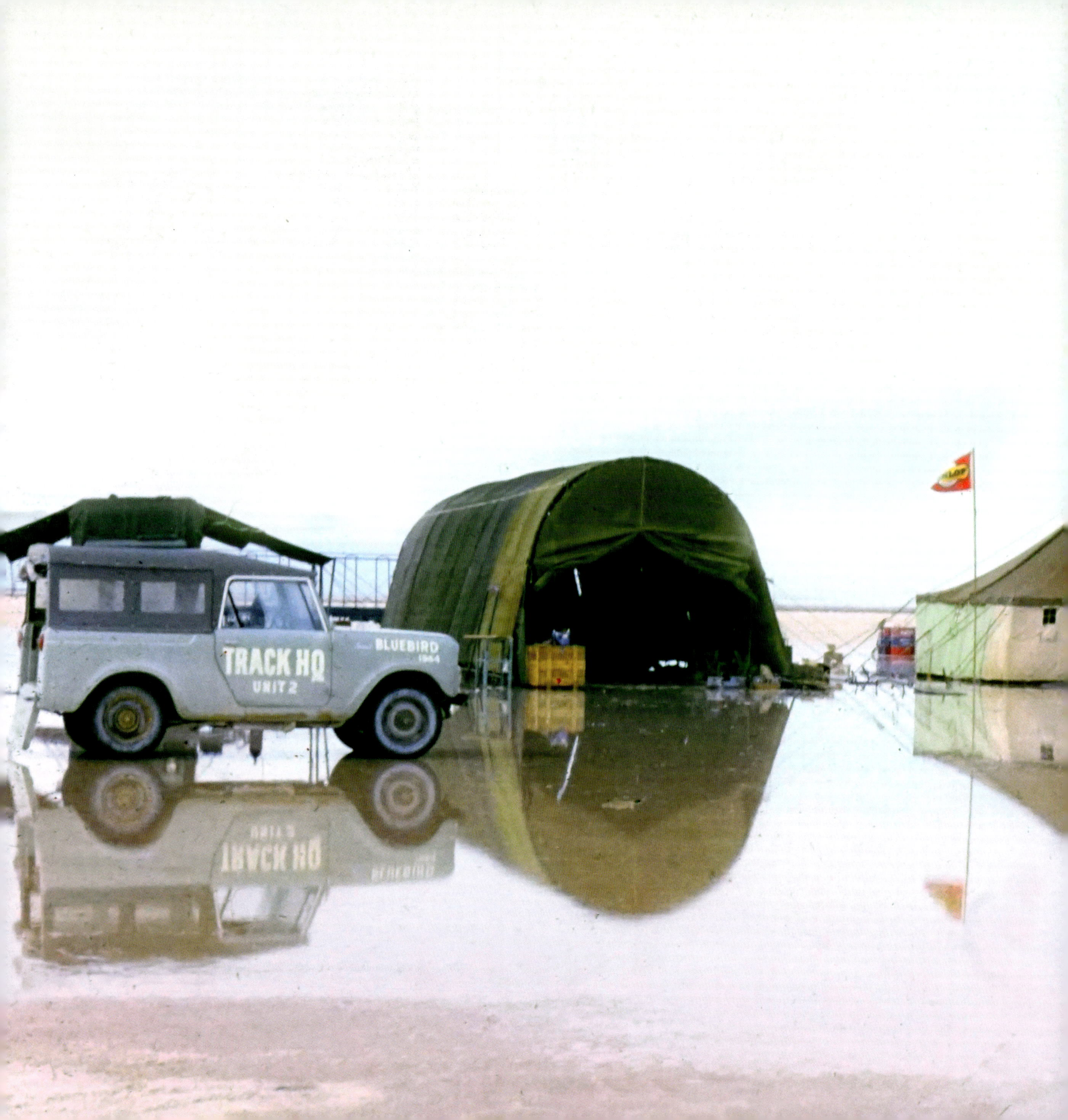
TRACK HQ
UNIT 2
BLUEBIRD
1964

Past the Point of no Return
1964–1967

Lake Eyre or bust 1964

Finally the team was back on Lake Eyre, albeit with a greatly reduced budget. BP had been prepared to keep the door open as a sponsor, but on terms which did not suit the Skipper; they eventually dropped out to be replaced by Ampol, the Australia fuel company and W.D. & H.O. Wills, makers of the finest cigarettes and ready rubbed tobacco, and Donald sold his Piper Apache twin-engined aircraft, registered G-APJL, for £12,500, as seen, flown and approved, to the Noarlunga Sand Pit Ltd, Adelaide.

In 1963 Craig Breedlove, a young American dragster racer, had done 417 mph at Bonneville in his three-wheeled jet-car, Spirit of America, which he had designed himself and built in his backyard on a shoestring. The sniping press received for the 1963 campaign also had its repercussions with Bluebird becoming an embarrassment to British industry. Stirling Moss, a racing driver and would-be-champion, who had clocked up a couple of class records, piped up, publicly stating that the Skipper lacked the split-second timing of a racing driver. Sir Alfred Owen, who built Bluebird twice, fell out with Donald, announcing publicly that he personally held him responsible for not getting the record and accusing him of mismanagement; he also claimed that CN7 belonged to him and forbade that the car run again. Donald protested and told him in no uncertain manner where to get off, that he was merely a sponsor, and a lawsuit was threatened, but in the end it was settled out of court. Though the sponsors were paying the piper, they had no right to call the tune.

Ron Wills from Bristol Siddeley, Maurie, Ken, Leo, George Hammond (Bristol's), Brian and Andrew Mustard (kneeling).

The biggest job was getting Bluebird cleaned up; the bodywork and the circuitry were in a mess and the engine became difficult to start. Meanwhile, work on the track progressed but conditions remained problematic even though the residual water on the lake surface disappeared quicker than anticipated, in fact at twice the evaporation rate normal for that time of the year as the salt crust was acting as a sponge while the main water table rose by some 4 inches. Conditions out on the lake remained treacherous. Bluebird's trailer broke through the crust; within a hundred yards it broke through again and then so did a lorry but eventually we got her to the hangar out on the salt.

The track team tried different methods to harden the surface but it never gave the adhesion required by the tyres: we were using Bluebird as a salt tester, not as a record breaker. On 28th May Donald finally did 352 mph with 70% power and looked ready to go, but then strong winds started to gust again and Bluebird was blown 18 feet off course. Days passed without the wind abating and when it did the track was in such bad condition, rutted, bumpy and mushy, that the team had to stand down for several weeks.

Every evening there was a meeting with the press: we'd had a rotten day, we'd been up since 4 a.m., out on the salt at first light, waited there all day, had one run and that was it, the wind was too strong ... Donald would come into the meeting; of course he looked a bit tired and haggard, of course he was feeling disconsolate, but nevertheless he always behaved well towards the team and the press. And, yes, he did put the spur into the team to carry on, he could do that, and they wanted to go on; they would never let him down.

By July the track had been repaired and the course graded but it rained again and one end of the track was now under 3 inches of water, reducing it by a precious 3 miles of acceleration and braking. By 14th July Donald had managed 320 and decided to call in the stewards and Longines from Adelaide to time the runs.

Ken Norris

Les Girls at the first base camp. Crystal, Vicky, Kier, Joan, Tonia and Rosemary.

Ken Reaks from Smiths Instruments would run up to Bluebird and switch on the recorders just as Don was about to pull off to save on the black box batteries.

Has he got the bottle?

We went through track after track, we went through rain after rain and we were fast running out of time. We had to have something to run on and that left us with Hobson's choice track which ran across a previous damaged track about 5 miles in. So when Donald made his record runs he accelerated for 5 miles, running over this wicked patch in the middle and then another 5 miles to halt, turning round and coming right back over it again.

Finally Donald had made his first really fast run at just over 400. We turned Bluebird around, jacked her up, changed the wheels, checked the gearbox oil temperatures and got him underway again as quickly as possible within the hour, but he was looking rather grim and grey sitting in the cockpit. While he was staring blankly up at the canopy he took a deep breath, smiled and then it seemed all his tension had been released. Later, I did ask him what had happened.

Ken Norris

Then we got the OK that the course was clear and off he went again, arriving at the other end safely to find that the tyres had been torn to ribbons and that his speed was far from what he had anticipated doing. The target speed was the 450 mph that the car would have done easily had the conditions been right. At least he had achieved what he set out to do. It had taken us a long time, a lot of money and a lot of disappointment.

Ken Norris

Dunlop Corner

The tyres got one hell of a beating: the entire thin rubber surface was peeled off them and Donald had been running on the cords. The adhesion material providing the thrust was gone. We got a 403 record and a sad Donald came of the cockpit; he brightened when he learnt he got 403 mph, but felt we deserved the 450 we wanted. We would have been happy with 450, but we never got back to that stage again.

Ken Norris

Ken my old lad, I nearly killed myself on that first run I was so close to going out of control it was funny. While I was sitting in that cockpit I thought I'd had it. I knew the second run would be worse, and as I gazed up I saw my father reflected in the canopy, looking down on me, as clear as I can see you now, and what he said to me was even clearer; 'Now my boy, now you know how I felt that day at Utah in 1935 when the tyre caught fire.' He broke out into quite broad grin, paused and then said, 'But don't worry old boy, it'll be alright!

Donald Campbell

Adelaide

The Australian people were still 100% behind Donald and he got the sort of reception in Adelaide he'd been used to in the States: they had organised a victory parade through the centre of town and Donald drove Bluebird at 35 mph with the canopy off. Donald, Tonia and Leo met Mayor Irwin and took luncheon with him and Mrs Irwin in the town hall. Over 200,000 people turned out to cheer Campbell-Bluebird, the streets were lined ten deep!

Donald's dissatisfaction with the record was profound. He had only bettered John Cobb's 1947 land speed record by 9 mph and the whole venture had cost over £1,000,000, and it got worse: in 1964 a magnificent jet-car battle broke out on the salt flats between Craig Breedlove (SOA), Art Arfons (Green Monster) and Tom Green (Wingfoot Express).

However, Donald was not down and out yet; and he came back in a way that only a Campbell could. We were going after the water speed record and the Double in Australia before the end of 1964.

Ken Norris

161

Barmera – Southern Australia

We left Adelaide for Barmera by road with Bluebird K7 and a spare jet engine; Barmera is 150 miles from Adelaide in an irrigated area growing grapes, apricots, peaches and citrus fruits and was originally established after the First World War as a settlement for ex-soldiers. It lies in the Riverland area on the shores of Lake Bonney. The lake was 4 miles long and 3 miles wide with a depth of 18 feet. Although the Skipper put in a number of runs, conditions were never satisfactory and the fastest he achieved was 216 mph. By 8th December, Donald decided to pull out and look for another lake.

Leo Villa

Brian Caddy was a former speed car and race boat driver and the president of the Barmera Water Ski Club. He was asked to provide support for the Bluebird team; his main role was to pilot the command boat with Leo and a police scuba-diver, Peter Pedro Warman, on board. They would be stationed in the middle of the course to monitor water conditions and advise Donald when to make his runs. Endless days were spent in the middle of Bonney in extreme heat.

Our day would start at 2.30 a.m. with breakfast at Gertie Bishop's café. Gertie, hair in rollers, in her dressing gown and fluffy slippers, would serve the Bluebird team bacon, sausage, beans, fried slice and three eggs whilst waiting for the latest weather report from the Bureau of Meteorology. If conditions were favourable, we would report to our respective posts and prepare for a run or two.

Inclement weather plagued the operations until 23rd November and as we were about to leave that morning a newspaper reporter handed me his camera saying, 'Brian, just point the camera and shoot as much as you can!' That is how this photo of Bluebird came about and it wasn't until 2013 that I saw it for the first time.

Brian's photo, 23rd November 1964.

On this high-speed run, Donald headed Bluebird straight for our boat at over 200 knots; I glanced over at Leo, who had a frown on his face and the perpetual W.D. & H.O. Wills' Woodbine hanging off his lower lip. I then felt our boat move and turned to see Pedro suited up, ready to dive overboard. I had been looking through the camera and hadn't realised how close Bluebird was to us, but I could see a devilish glint in Donald's eyes as plain as the nose on my own face as he sped past us less than 50 feet away. I knew then that Don was relaxed and ready to do business.

Sadly the elements were truly against us again; the snow had melted in the Snowy Mountains 500 miles away and the Murray River was flooding Lake Bonney. The rising water was forced into Bonney through Nappers Bridge. The flood water was creating a wave of pressure running north to south which was not visible to the naked eye, but when Bluebird was running at over 200 mph she was bouncing across the top of the water every 50 yards; it was like a car bumping along a corrugated dirt road so we changed lakes.

Joan Villa and Bunty Parfitt.

Dumbleyung - Western Australia

Approximately 13 kilometres long by 6.5 kilometres wide, its catchment area extends 64 km north to Kulin, 64 kilometres south to Gnowangerup and 55 kilometres east of Tarin Rock. Previously when it overflowed, the water ran through the Wagin Lakes into the Beaufort River, the Blackwood and then into the sea at Augusta. As a comparison, Lake Dumbleyung covers 5,200 hectares and the total tidal area of the Swan River is 5,300 hectares.

After some testing, Donald made his first early morning run, duck opening day, with ducks flying in all directions. Donald was fearful of having a bird or two sucked into the jet engine, and wrecking it and his chances of achieving the Double, so word was sent to the shire for the local game wardens, to see if there was a solution in moving the ducks away from the lake. Shots were fired but the ducks stubbornly remained; a couple of them were captured and sent to Perth to understand why they were not flying away from Bluebird.

Once again, the wind was making the lake too rough for a record attempt: it would blow early in the morning, and the Albany Doctor would come in from the south at about 3 p.m. and blow us completely off the lake. It was very frustrating and we were running out of time.

Brian Caddy, 2016

167

Floating platform for Bluebird's Lucas starter batteries. The divers are dealing with the tree stumps.

The bank had quite a steep incline down to the water even though the lake was meant to be some 5 or so feet higher than normal. Eventually we found a site suitable for launching and I paddled out, checked out the depth and said, 'Right boys, this will do.' The Dumbleyung crew were taken aback; how would we launch Bluebird without a ramp? It was very steep and there were dozens of dead Wattle tree trunks in the water blocking access to open water. I explained to the Shire that with a bulldozer and a Railway Track Gang we could build a ramp. However the trees remained a problem: how could we cut a hundred yard channel through them? Simple, get the West Australian Police Diving Team to cut the trees down under water on the bottom, then we could attach a pontoon to the stumps on the outer edge to carry Bluebird's starter batteries.

In 1964, such things were still possible.

As the logistics man for the World Water Speed Record attempt, I had only a week before K7 arrived on site. Graham Ferret, Donald's project manager, had left for Adelaide and left me to organise the base camp and facilities.

The next requirement was marker buoys for the course, and, as it happens, it was a period when 500-gallon fuel storage tanks were being introduced onto farms, and Ampol, the leading Australian fuel company and sponsor, had a yard full of them ready to be assembled. They became our buoys.

The base camp from where to manage operations, with living accommodation and toilets, a canteen and a cookhouse, was next. The locals kindly provided the caravans; the Australian Army provided tents, a canteen with cookhouse and a 240-volt generator. Then there was the Weston Australia duck season to contend with, which was opening in just a couple of weeks, right at the time that Donald would starting high-speed trials, so the Government declared Dumbleyung a sanctuary. My immediate reply was that, 'you will have all the ducks in Weston Australia on that lake,' and so it was.

Brian Caddy, 2016

Donald often ran Bluebird with a 16 mm Zap camera on board. On Dumbleyung he was shooting footage for his production, *How Long a Mile*.

Coming back in, 31st December 1964.

Bluebird headquarters and camp site.

169

We met with the Shire Council and the Water Ski Club and I explained that we had no use for a ramp as we had to avoid creating a wash across the lake, so we had to launch at one end and go straight down the middle to the other end, then turn, refuel, start up the Beryl and come back to where we had started, within one hour.

Brian Caddy, 2016

New Year's Eve, 1964

Champing at the bit, Donald called me on the radio: 'Come on Unc I'm all-ready. Don't mess about!'

It took all the determination in the world to reply, 'Hold it, Skipper, conditions not right!' while the others in the tender boat were urging me to let him go before a breeze sprung up. After another 5 minutes I called Donald with, 'Good luck. It's all yours Skipper!' We heard the good old Beryl start up and Donald saying 'She's underway,' and then silence, and then, 'Bollocks! I've stalled the bloody engine. Come on boys! Come over and start me up again! And make it bloody quick!'

In Australia there's no real twilight; at about 8.55 p.m. it's twilight and by 9.00 p.m. it's dead dark and you can't see a damned thing. I sat there, helpless, hoping, minutes ticking by, then the old Beryl fired up once again and Don flashed by us at an incredible speed, followed not long afterwards by both darkness and our old mate the Albany Doctor. So while we were making one hectic dash to get all the buoys off the lake, Donald was told by the Longines boys that he had now got his Double with a new water speed record of 276.3 mph. We were all so bloody elated, like hell we were! The Double!

This was, without any doubt, Donald's finest performance.

Leo Villa

Pussy Cat Hill, 31st December 1964.

Man of the people

'Donald was a thorough English gentleman. He was also a charming speaker with great wit. In Perth, after his demonstration run on the Swan River, he was happy to announce, 'I'm the man to have passed water the fastest under the Narrows Bridge.'

Angus Tuck was 18 when Donald visited his home one afternoon for tea to meet with his dad. Donald asked Angus if he would like join the Bluebird team as a general helper to Chief Engineer Leo Villa and Mechanic Maurie Parfitt, who were apparently getting on in years. The decision was taken to move to the west from Barmera with Angus driving the Woodies truck (containing the spare Beryl and all the spares).

School children were lined up in the streets of the towns of Wagin and Narrogin as we made our way to the lake. We drove in convoy down to Dumbleyung and set up camp in the caravans by the lake.

Windy weather was the problem and we spent December waiting for the right conditions. On calm days we were often beaten by the incoming Esperance Doctor, a breeze that would blow in mid-afternoon. On Christmas Day Donald flew back from Perth with a bundle of presents for his team, dressed as Father Christmas, and handed out gifts specially chosen for us all. In my case he knew that I was going to further studies the next year and presented me with a briefcase which I greatly treasured. They put on a wonderful all-day Christmas party in the Dumbleyung pub and Tonia was just fantastic, such a wonderful entertainer, singing great songs and telling us great stories.

On New Year's Eve it looked as though windy weather conditions would again thwart the attempt and Donald, Tonia and Graham Ferrett went up in the plane and whilst overflying the lake they noticed perfect conditions in the middle and raced back down to the Bluebird.

That evening, after breaking the record, Donald asked me to get everyone together and as a part of his thank you he presented me with his Bluebird overalls (currently on display in Barmera). Donald cared very much for the well-being of each member of his team.

On New Year's Eve it was champagne by the lake and next day we travelled to Perth for the Perth Cup Day at Ascot with team members parading in open cars around the race course. The Bluebird was transferred to the Royal Perth Yacht Club for demonstration runs on the Swan River. Donald always made sure that his team were included in the celebrations, including a civic reception and a visit to Government House, where Governor Sir Douglas Kendrew recieved us in his drawing room.

Donald flew back to Barmera later in January 1965 to express his thanks to the Barmera community. He touched the people of Barmera in many ways with his involvement in community activities and although he didn't actually break the world record here on Lake Bonney, I think we feel very much part of his journey to success on Dumbleyung in 1964. Donald was a very brave man who always knew that his next run might be his last.

Angus Tuck, 2016

'One of my tasks at Dumbleyung was to row Donald and Tonia out in a dingy to the pontoon where the Bluebird was moored. I remember those few minutes as being a quiet time with, I imagine, Donald and Tonia thinking about what lay ahead.'

Angus rowing Donald and Tonia out to Bluebird K7.

The Double

With three hours of daylight left on 31st December, Donald had brought off his Double and he became the first man to break the water and land speed records in the same year. This was without any doubt Donald's finest achievement; alas, we did not realise at the time but it would be his last. On New Year's Day Donald, Tonia, Joan and I flew to Perth and were entertained by Sir Douglas Kendrew, Governor of Western Australia, at Ascot Race Course, where we watched the famous Perth Gold Cup Races. Donald later gave a few demo runs on the estuary of the Swan River in Perth. Bluebird K7 was eventually handed over to Ampol to be displayed at their petrol stations across Australia. The team flew back home and Donald stayed on to post-produce his film *How Long a Mile*, shot by Ajax Films.

Leo Villa

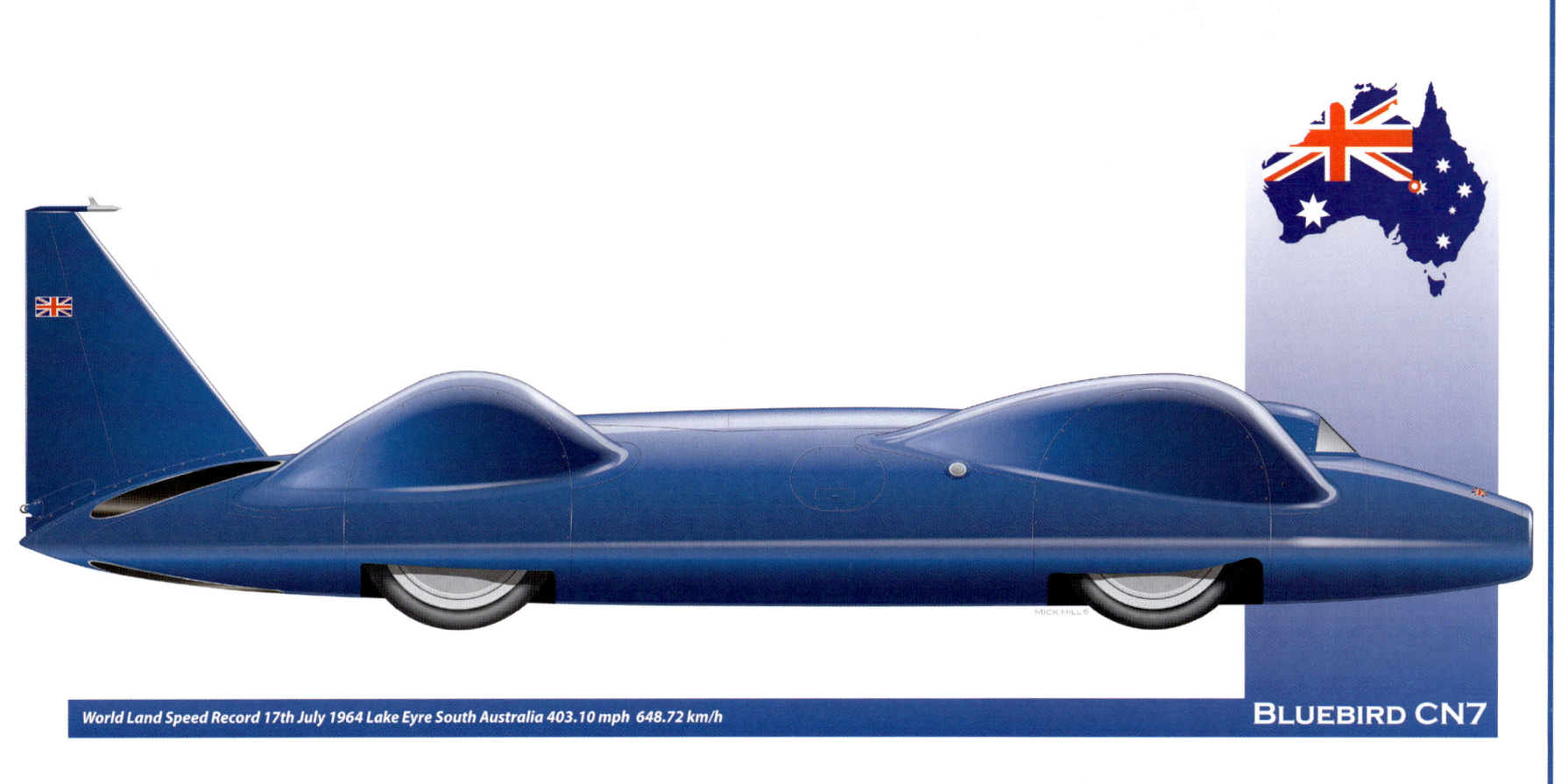

World Land Speed Record 17th July 1964 Lake Eyre South Australia 403.10 mph 648.72 km/h

BLUEBIRD CN7

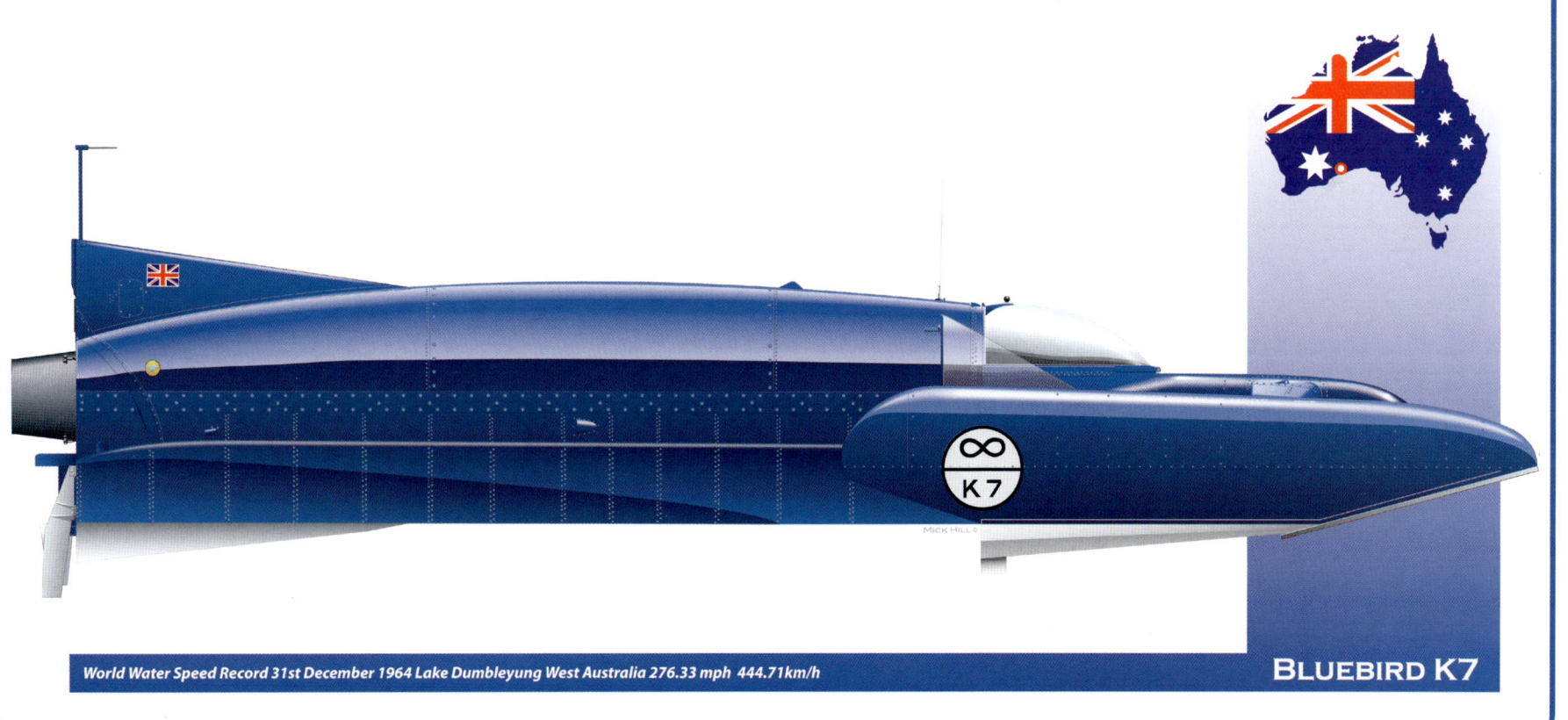

World Water Speed Record 31st December 1964 Lake Dumbleyung West Australia 276.33 mph 444.71km/h

BLUEBIRD K7

Timing the Bluebirds

Longines started timing the Bluebirds in 1937 with stopwatches, when Malcolm broke the water speed record in Switzerland three times. Their equipment was used until 1967 by the Campbells; more often than not the team from St Imier would undertake the timings.

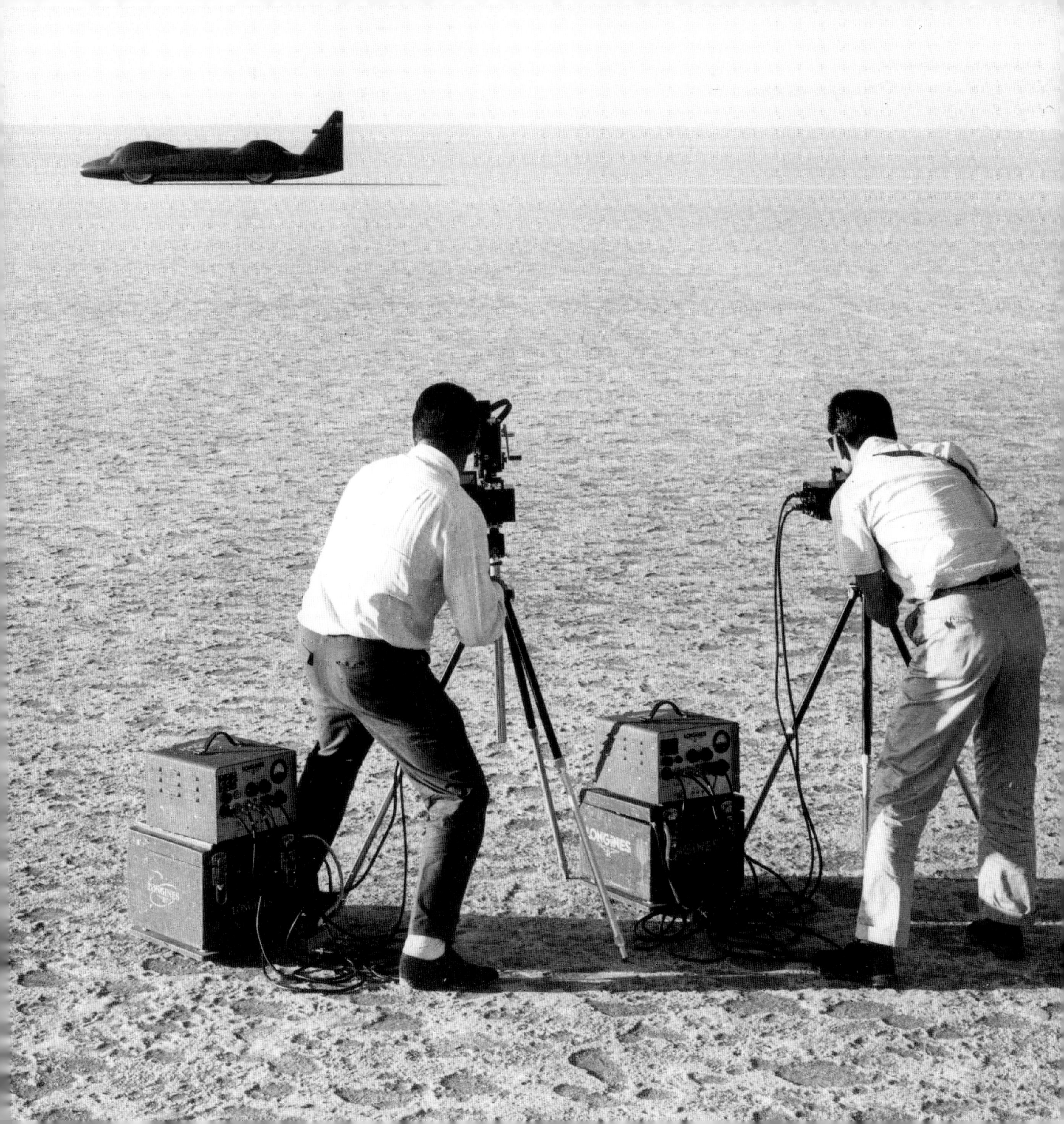
LONGINES

... and for my next trick

Following the Double, the burning question was what to do next? Ken suggested either to build one vehicle to break both land and water records or to go supersonic on land ... What else?

August 1966, at home at Priors Ford.

The sound barrier at sea level: CN8

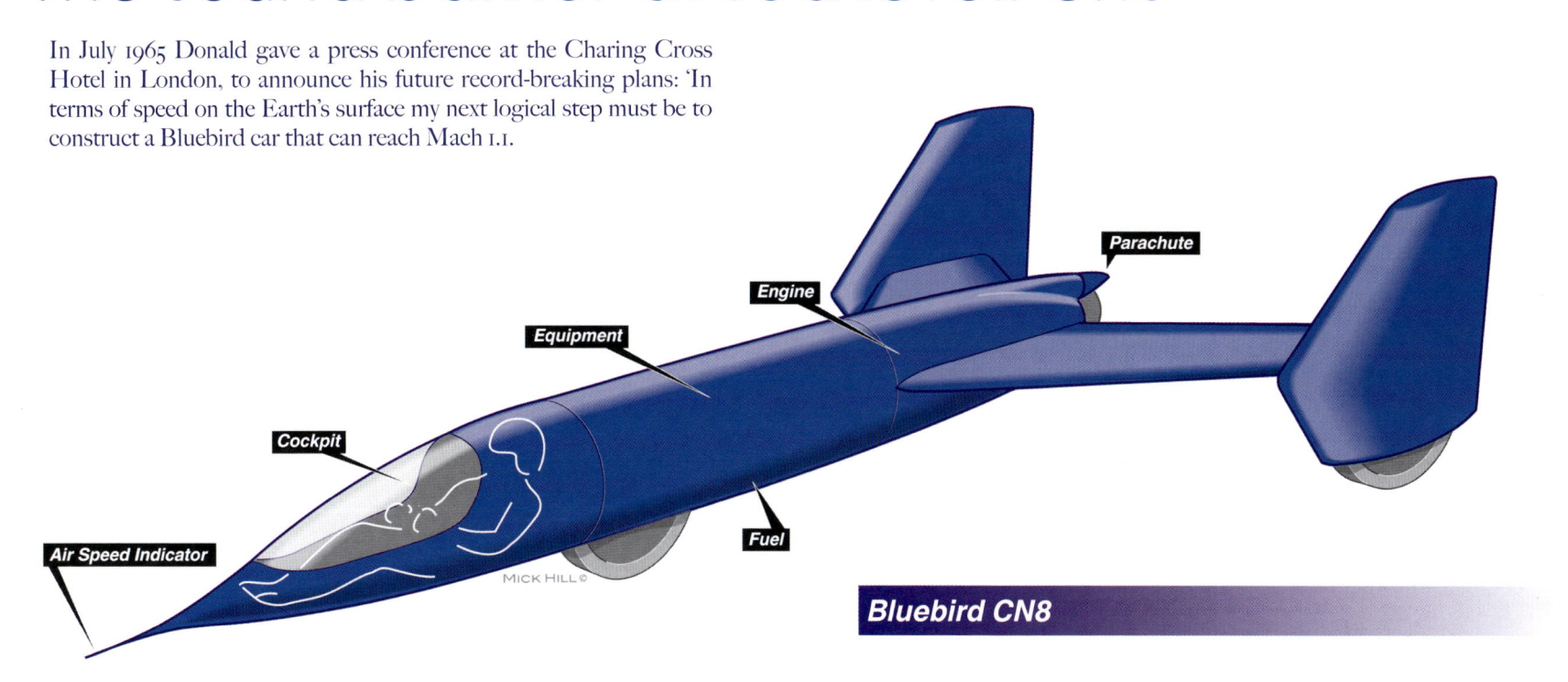

In July 1965 Donald gave a press conference at the Charing Cross Hotel in London, to announce his future record-breaking plans: 'In terms of speed on the Earth's surface my next logical step must be to construct a Bluebird car that can reach Mach 1.1.

Bluebird CN8

The Americans are already making plans for such a vehicle and it would be tragic for the world image of British technology if we do not compete in this great contest and win. Make no mistake, the nation whose technologists are first to seize the faster than sound record on land will be the nation whose industry will be seen to leapfrog into the seventies or eighties. We can have it on the track in three years.'

Donald Campbell

Ken designed a simple chassis with one rocket engine up top, one underneath and it was of the pencil design with a slim body to interact less with shockwaves, a favourite configuration in the seventies (Blue Flame – Budweiser). A mock-up was made and presented at a sponsorship day at Priors Ford in 1966, with K7 and CN7 on display.

But Donald got no interest at all.

1964 – US jet-cars

Bluebird had been designed for speeds up to 600 mph in 1958.

The Wingfoot Express, 413.12 mph, on 2nd October.

The Green Monster, 536.02 mph, on 4th November.

The Spirit of America, 468.72 mph, on 5th November. 526.28 mph, on 13th November.

179

1966 – The Magic 300 Mark

Donald to generate support for CN8 300+ on water seemed like a cheap, quick, fix-it. When he announced his intention Tonia and Leo responded poorly. Lew told Donald outright he would kill himself, not even to contemplate it and wait a couple of years Norris Brothers would build him a new boat.

Behind the cattle market in Haywards Heath

To keep costs to a minimum the conversion was entrusted to Norris Brothers Ltd personnel and a large wooden shed was erected in the car park at their premises on Burrell Road. Dust free conditions were maintained in the shed by covering the floor with a concrete sealer of epoxy resign. As always with Campbell-Bluebird, expertise, materials, equipment and components were forthcoming free of charge and quickly thirty firms, including Bristol-Siddeley and Smiths instruments were involved.

K7's new performance requirements for the 4.5 mile Coniston course

- A record speed of 300 + with a safe maximum operating speed of up to 325 mph
- Installation of the more powerful and lighter Bristol-Siddeley Orpheus jet engine
- Safety factors and taxiing speed: no less than with the Beryl installation
- Planing to be reached with no more difficulty than with the Beryl
- A run each way without refuelling with 3-4 on-board air starts

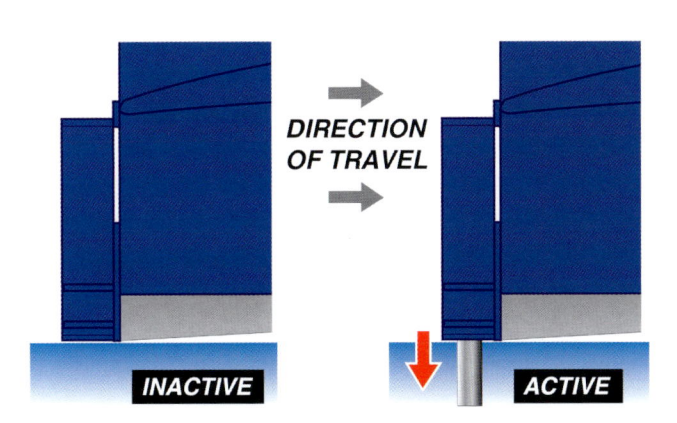

Water brake

Still being preoccupied with the length of Coniston, a water brake was part of Bluebird's refit. It was composed of a metal ram, 4 inches square (opposite, directly below the red engine cowl), actuated hydraulically from the cockpit. When lowered into the water behind the hydroplane's rear planing shoe, the brake would generate about 5,000 lb of drag, reducing speed rapidly.

Orpheus

To reach the magic 300 mark on the short Coniston course, Bluebird required more thrust and power to get up to speed faster. The final engine fitted to Bluebird had a booster fuel system and was running at 110%, providing about 5,250 lb of thrust. The weight and length difference of the new engine caused significant balancing problems and it was only after weeks of heartbreak and toil that the boat began to plane.

Spray deflectors not plastic 'blinker' shields

Engine air intakes: intake plastic blinker shields, we have been considering this and feel that a much larger portion of the new 1.5-inch-radius intake lip can be made available to ingest air during low-speed acceleration if they are re-examined as water spray deflectors and not blinkers. The object is redirect the impinging spray as distinct from covering up the intake to keep the spray out. Apart from reducing the level of the upper part of the plastic intake shield to enable the upper two thirds of the intake lip to freely ingest air in the low-speed range, it would seem if the plastic shield was reshaped as a deflector plate (see diagram), then the remaining upper third of the intake can play its part without masking from the shield. This is achieved simply by bolting, bracketing and the use of hot water to reshape the deflectors on the job.

Memo LH/NWS/16134, to Mr E Ravenhill, Norris Brother Ltd, dated 8th August 1966, from Bristol Siddeley Engines Ltd, signed N.W. Sharp, Chief Installation Engineer.

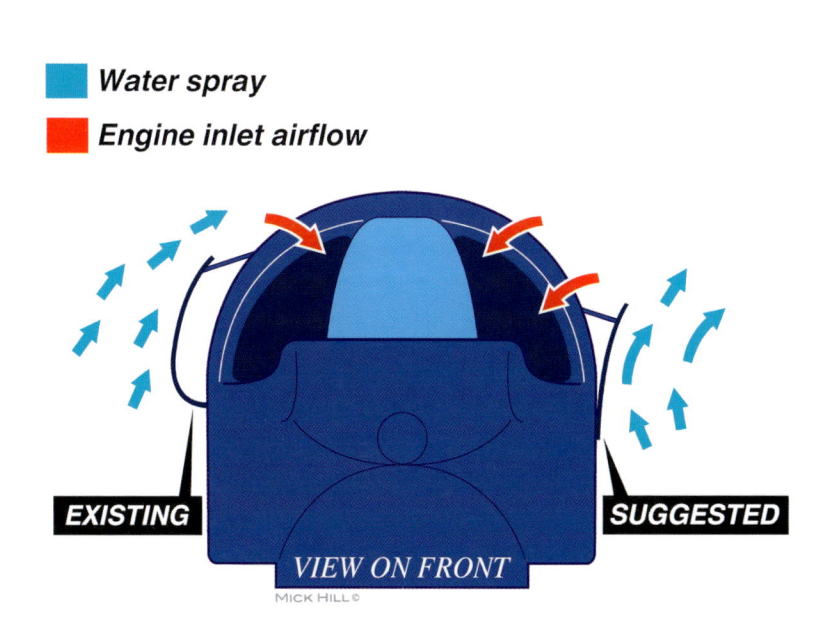

4th January 1967 Coniston Water

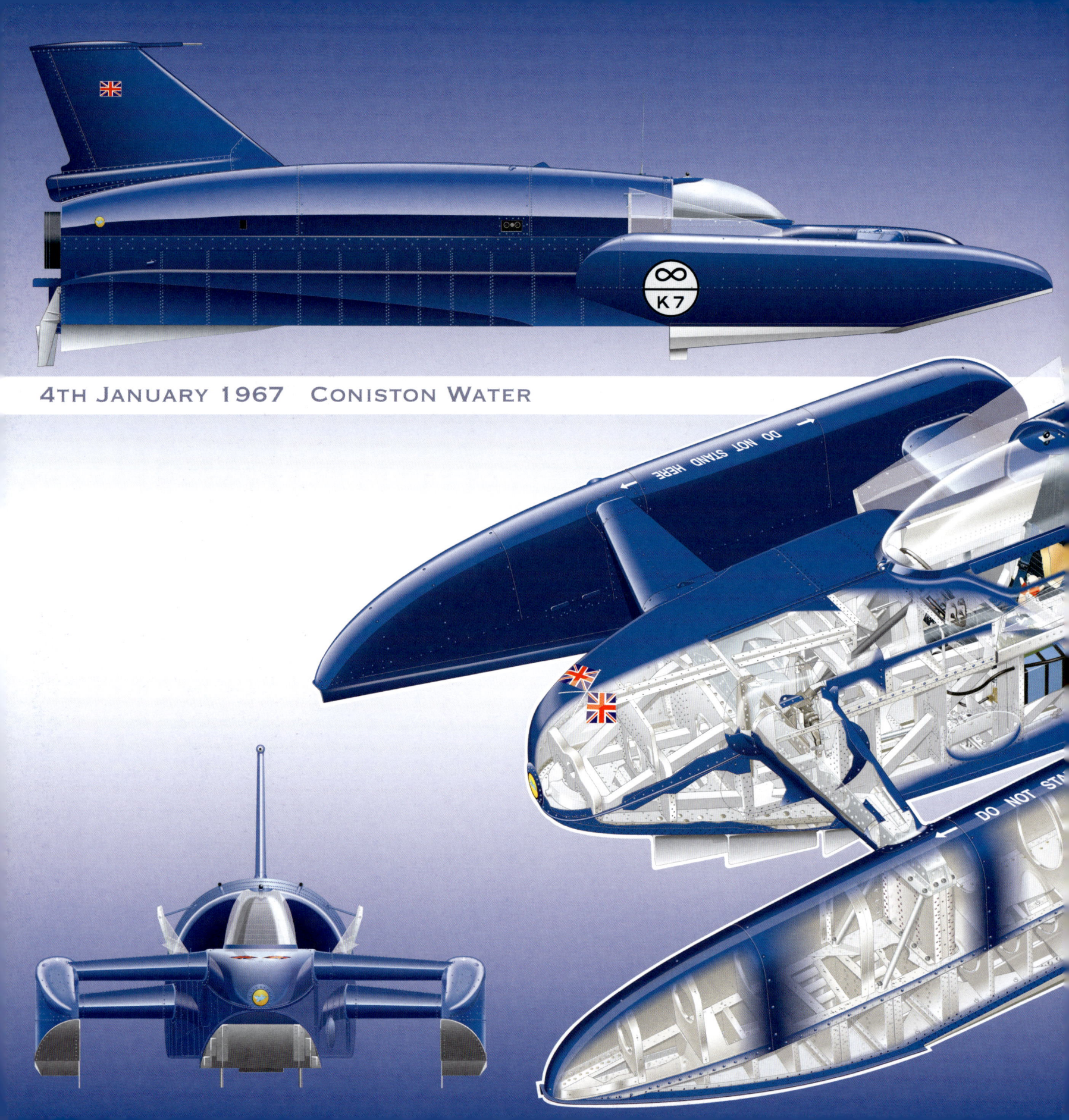

DO NOT STAND HERE

DO NOT STAND HERE

∞
K7

What a stubborn bugger

Don's determination and stubbornness were as great as ever and his perspective of the situation is truer today than it was in 1966: 'The team that built Bluebird and have carried out the modifications would be my answer to anyone who says speed records are out of date. Given the backing, these are the sorts of British engineers who could work on imaginative space projects. But do we in this country have a chance of getting any proper programme of this kind backed?'

Mrs Connie Robinson

Donald arrived at Coniston on 3rd November. Connie Robinson was again accommodating the team at The Sun Inn; she, her son Robbie and the hotel staff became part of the team for the duration. When the Campbells were in town it was a family affair.

711

During a full-power test of Bluebird's new Orpheus, the air intakes collapsed, unable to meet the demands of the more powerful jet ingesting the rivets it was writtenoff. The team with added specialists worked by the freezing lakeside in a tarpaulin-clad boathouse to change the engine over for the spare. The intakes were modified and strengthened at Bourners and refitted to Bluebird. During initial trials large amounts of water were thrown up, putting out the engine, the old spray baffles now being inadequate; various designs were fitted, but none was successful until the set designed by Bristol Siddeley Ltd were made and fitted. They worked perfectly.

Problems

What are my feelings? These difficulties are nothing new. They have happened over and over again since I first started trying to beat records sixteen years ago. The ability of our team with their unique skill and unrivalled technical know-how has given us a commanding lead. I am sure that sheer guts and determination will keep them working around the clock, in the biting Coniston north-east wind, to put this setback behind us. I feel justified in being both patient and confident...

Donald, *Daily Sketch*, November 1966

Anything for the Skipper

Donald's hands-on approach got people involved in his projects; with his charm and charisma he would motivate and encourage them to undertake tasks that they would normally not do. Skilled individuals and companies would help out because Donald was prepared to do things himself; he was always there leading the project. He was natural and relaxed; he would not always give a direct order but get people to undertake tasks by suggestion. 'It would be a good idea if you could so such and such 'ole boy!' 'They work with me, not for me; it's the cause that counts!'

Leo down by the seaside reading his post. Late November 1966, fitting the spray deflectors in their final form.

Full power static test of the new Orpheus, Ken Norris to the left, Don and Bill Vanryne of Rotax, the air starter specialist.

Tramping like mad

Bluebird required mirror-like conditions on the lake to run safely at full speed and all the more in her final 'sprint' configuration.

Donald would take Bluebird out as often as the weather permitted, even for just short runs, but after several weeks no worthwhile improvements resulted from the many modifications. Donald probably didn't expect them to do otherwise. The days of waiting had become weeks and a man waiting a test of his courage wanted more than *just* to sit at the water's edge awaiting its pleasure. The warmth and comfort of the Sun Inn was an oasis as the temperature slowly kept on falling and the snow line crept further and further down the Old Man of Coniston with each successive day.

Donald had the ability to get everybody to pull together under difficult circumstances. It never occurred to them not to get along with him; maybe because the challenge was greater, the team pulled even harder. All those that worked closely with him will say the same; it was as simple as that. You never thought, 'why am I doing this?' You were part of a small, tight-knit, dedicated team with one single aim: to get another successful World Speed Record. That was it!

Robbie

We're back in business

With bags of sand attached to her stern to move the centre of balance back, Robbie and Leo in the Dory look on as Donald puts the power on. Note the 'spray deflectors'.

Donald and I had gone to the greengrocers for some potato sacks and, as it turned out, he had a big heap of sand in the backyard, so I just used that and weighed them on the scales he'd use for a hundredweight of potatoes or corn. We put 56 lb in each sack. I filled them and weighed them whilst the rest went back for breakfast and then we went back to the boathouse and tied them on to the back of Bluebird with rope.

The Dory closed, gathered the tow rope and then moved over to her flank. The growing whine of the Orpheus could be clearly heard from the bank as Donald started to open her up from the northern end, but this time the foam at the bow dwindled – disappeared – *she was planing!*

Robbie

The lazy ripples of danger

Weights had been cast from ingots of lead and fitted into Bluebird's stern for the desired balance by moving the centre of gravity back a few inches. Planing for the first time, Donald starts high speed trials late in 1966.

One of the most impressive feelings I had about Donald was that he would not put his foot down until everything was absolutely right and then when he did put his foot down he really went for it! There was no question of it on Lake Coniston. If you consider that lake: it is about 4.5 miles long (5 km) and half a mile wide. So we went down to a flying kilometre, with 6 kilometres in all, 3 either side of the centre, but 2.5 to entry and 2.5 at the exit. So Donald had to accelerate up to 300 mph in 2.5 km and then he had to decelerate in 2.5 km and there is a right-handed bottleneck between Peel Island on the left and the rocks on the right. You can't have the boat off track, it has got to be right in the middle, at 200 knots plus the water brake goes in before you slow enough to enter the bay turn refuel or stop. Then you have to come back the other way and do the same thing. So you've got to go for it, but, my God, when it was needed for Donald to go for it – he did. It was frightening – when you really heard the power go on! You just crossed your fingers.

Lew Norris

Full power

0 mph: Close to the pier you push the starter button and then the air-starter takes over, fires the engine and in about 3 seconds you're away very slowly.

15 mph: A critical moment. Watch the jet pipe temperature, too much power and the water will flood the engine. Line up on track.

25 mph: Bluebird's nose lifts off the water. Very difficult stage with huge amounts of water flying up all over the front of the engine.

40 mph: Still accelerating with caution, rear planing shoe still down.

70 mph: Another critical moment requiring a very delicate manoeuvre: brake; turn left sharply to unstick the back of the boat from the water.

Up comes the rear shoe and she's away!

In 9 seconds up to 300 mph with about 14 inches of Bluebird touching the water. Then braking begins. If you just cut the engine it would take 3.5 miles to stop. We have only 2 miles and a tricky S-bend to negotiate. I am hoping nothing will go wrong at this stage. When you slow with the new brake the stern drops at about 80. Each time clouds of water obscure all vision and you are blinded. You either sink into the water by reducing speed further, hoping you are pointing in the right direction or remain in the taxiing position dropping only the rear shoe keeping the bows up. But by then the adrenaline is really pumping around the cockpit and you're ready for that return run. This is only what one *expects* to happen. All we know is that Bluebird's new set-up works on paper. It's up to me to find out if it works on water.

Our man from St Imier

They all raised their glasses in the village of Coniston last night and drank a toast to Old Father Time. It was his 66th birthday. At that moment Raoul Crelerot had his stopwatch on a game of darts in the Sun Hotel. Not that that is his main mission at Coniston. For Raoul is head of the team of professional timekeepers from Longines, the Swiss watch company. They're here to time Donald Campbell's World Water Speed Record bid on Coniston Water. Time is Raoul's business and he has travelled thousands of miles round the world to record, with indisputable accuracy, the occasions that have made sporting history. He will slip over to Brazil for a cycle race, then time a regatta in Czechoslovakia, or it could be the world skiing championships in Chile. He spends only about ten weekends in the year at his home in Switzerland. 'Time,' says Raoul, 'means everything to me.' That's why he is keeping a lonely vigil at Coniston on a wooden pier at one end of the measured kilometre over which Donald Campbell will soon be making his record bid with two timed runs.

All set for the record

Around him is set-up some of the £10,000' worth of special equipment Longines have designed and developed and taken there to time the record. The special, high-speed Bolex cameras and the quartz-crystal clocks are in position. The watches actuated by electro mechanical impulses are set. Raoul, and his colleagues at the other end of the kilometre course, amuse themselves by testing their equipment on boats on the lake and cars on the roads. If something moves they can time it. One of Longines' directors, Doctor Luc Niggli, flew over from Switzerland just to spend the day at Coniston with his team and said, 'We donate our timekeeping services for projects like this so that there can be no dispute afterwards.'

When Donald Campbell makes his runs; the timekeepers will have his speed just about as quickly as the run itself. Within seconds of Campbell crossing the line, his speed in miles per hour will be radioed to Bluebird's cockpit. It will also be handed to the official observer, Mr Norman Buckley, representing the world governing body of World Water Records, the Royal Yachting Association.

It will take a brave man to dispute the figure with Old Father Time ...
Brian Boss, 1966

Raoul Crelerot, Longines' chief timekeeper from St Imier, with the Chronocinégines and the back-up electronically triggered stop watches.

Donald had told a group of pressmen that they had come up to Coniston to see him break his neck, not the record. 'You've only come here to see me turn the bloody boat over on its back!' The remark had lingered amongst the team and haunted them every time they looked at him. Why did he have to do it? What drove him to yet one more excursion into a lonely screaming hell of his own making?

Another morning

6.30 a.m. Donald looked out on a starlight sky; there was no movement in the air through the open window of the bungalow. He dressed and breakfasted. Back in the Sun Inn, whilst the customary coffee and toast were being served, Donald pressed the starter button of his blue E-type and weaved his way down to the boathouse. Bluebird's shelter was already ablaze, the water was excellent and there was not a sound to be heard, no lapping water, no waves, no wind.

Preparations went ahead and Bluebird was slipped into the water. Donald prepared himself, communicated with his team by radio and then hit the starter button. You could hear your heartbeat as a distant hum away to the north grew slowly to a roar and then a rumble, which closed rapidly with its ensuing echo as Bluebird came into sight and she swept across the lake and was instantly gone. The familiar triangular fin of spray dispersed with the sound waves.

Andrew Brown gave Bluebird's coded speed message over the radio which was patched through a loudspeaker for the pressmen.

Message for Skipper - + 47 - + 47 (code: 297 mph = 250 + 47)
Message for Skipper from Tango +47 - + 47

Surprisingly Bluebird returned after just a few moments! Donald hadn't stopped or refuelled. The sound of the jet thundered across the water as she appeared again in the morning haze from behind Peel Island, this time even faster.

This run was even faster than the first; Bluebird was now barely touching the water as she entered the timing sector, rapidly shrinking three patches of white spray pinpointing her position - that was unusual, the wake was cut. They stared as if hypnotised rather than in horror as Bluebird slowly rose into the air ... and over the radio ..."I've gone!" She turned over slowly on her back then plunged steeply into the water as a tremendous column of spray rose and hung like a curtain as the frenzied somersaults could be seen through the thrashing water. She lay still for just a second as a last breath of steam went up. Then she too was gone! The remaining spray thinned and then the surface settled.

Not a word was uttered. Up the lake the support boats were already moving to the scene with dear ol' Leo - Une - who had shared all of Donald's joys, all of his tribulations throughout his 47-year life.

Dear old Leo, to whom fate had been so cruel in withholding its hand to ensure that his grim severance from his dearly beloved Skipper should happen right in front of his very eyes.

An anguished cry in the distance went out: 'Oh! No! Oh! No!' it drifted across the lake and then silence, except that this time there was no peace - except for him.

Ted Hamel, 1967

The conditions that morning were right, but deteriorating. From the weather report we knew he had to go then or call it off for the day. In fact minutes after the crash the wind came up and it would have been impossible for him to go at all. Donald knew that every run was a calculated risk and he was prepared to take that risk.

Keith Harrison

The lake had no time to settle from the first run and Donald did not get Bluebird on the right track. There is no doubt he hit his own wash. K7 had a maximum three degrees lift before it would fly, they always knew that. It was an error of judgement forced by the weather, within minutes of the crash the lake was unusable.

Andy Brown

I was at the lake between Christmas and the New Year. The night before he was killed I had to leave Donald and go South. I told him 'we knew he couldn't run this week and the weather would break for the weekend and I'd be back.' He said to me: 'Don't go! Tomorrow, I assure you, it will all be over!'

Ken Norris

You had to do the return run within an hour and it would very rarely stay stable for an hour, so Donald developed the technique of running very fast and back the other way within 2 or 3 minutes while the surface was settled. It was Ken and I's conclusion that on the run back, when he had the accident, he tracked a little too near the coast, he had to track much more quickly, he had to turn

04/01/67

GMT 08.40

'Leo, Leo, How's your water? OVER'
There appear to be no birds in the way at the moment, and there is a slight down swell on the water, but it could be caused by our own boat..
OVER

'Kilo, we are underway
[21 second pause]
OK Leo do you read me? OVER'

GMT 08.45

Coming in loud and clear Skipper ...
Coming in loud and clear

Two bloody swans have just taken-off going down the lake, 'I'm underway, all systems normal; brake swept up, er ... air pressure warning light on.. coming onto track now and er ... I'll open up as soon as I am heading down the lake, er doesn't look too smooth from here, doesn't matter, here we go ... Here we go ...

[3 second pause]

... Passing through four ... five coming up...

a lot of water, nose beginning to lift ...

water all over the front of the engine again ... and the nose is up ... low pressure fuel ...warning light ... going left

OK we're up and away ... and passing through er ... tramping very hard at 150 ... very hard indeed ... FULL POWER ... Passing through 2 ... 25 out of the way ... I don't think I can get over the top, but I'll try,

FULL HOUSE ... and I can't see where I am ...
FULL HOUSE FULL HOUSE - FULL HOUSE ... POWER OFF NOW ...
I'M THROUGH!! ...

Full Power ... there! ...
passing through 25 ... Peel Island ... passing through 2 ..

I'm lighting like mad ... brake gone down...engine lighting up now ... relighting ... passing Peel Island... relight made normal ... and the bow ... down ... down now ... passing through 100 ... nose hasn't dropped yet ... nose down ... Leo, do you read me? OVER

Hello ... read you Skipper ...come in
16 second long static
'Base do you read me? OVER'
Reading you Skipper, come in...
'Base, will you get a message from Tango please? OVER
Base, Roger, in actual fact that was Alpha that answered you Skipper. OVER ...
'Don't worry about Alpha! I want a message from Tango. OVER ...

Donald Campbell (Call Sign: Skipper)
Leo Villa – Course controller (Call Sign: Alpha)
Stephen Darbishire – Timekeepers (Call Sign: Tango)
Paul Evans – Communications (Call Sign: Base)

Roger Skipper ... Tango. Tango do you read? OVER
Tango to Base, Tango to Base ... Stand-by ...
[Static]
Tango to Base - Tango to Base ... Message for Skipper ... +47 +47 +47 ... do you copy that? Repeat OVER
ROGER - ROGER - ROGER ... Base for Skipper. Base for Skipper, from Tango, +47 +47 OVER

'Roger Paul... I'm starting the return run now

[21 second pause with 8 second static]

GMT 08.48

Full nose up ... Pitching a bit down here, coming through our own wash and er getting straightened up now on track ... rather closer to Peel Island ... and we're tramping like mad

FULL POWER ...
tramping like hell OVER ...
I can't see much and the water's very bad indeed ...

can't get over the top ...

I'm getting a lot of bloody row in here ...

I can't see anything ...

I've got the bows up

I've gone

[32 seconds transmission]
Hello ...Tango to Base, Tango to Base OVER

Base to Tango OVER...Base to Tango OVER...
Tango to Base ...Tango To Base ...
Complete accident I'm afraid ... OVER
Er, roger, er details? OVER
No details as yet, no details ...

'He was a man, take him for all in all,
We shall not look upon his like again'

William Shakespeare, Hamlet; Act 1, Scene 2

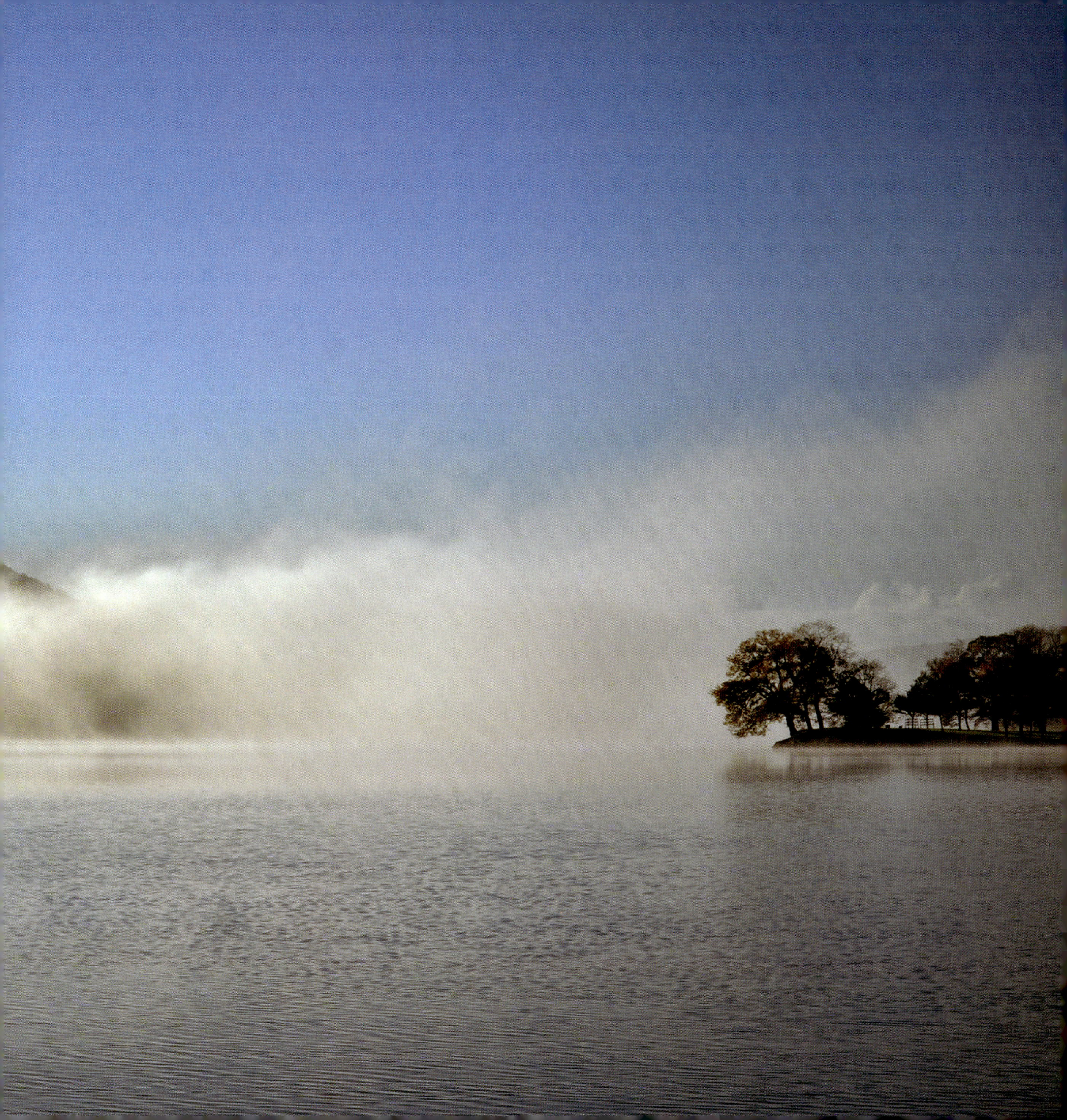

Of Men and Machines

Spirit of Australia I

On 8th October 1978, Australian Ken Warby, in his jet-powered, unlimited class hydroplane, Spirit of Australia, took the World Water Speed Record for the second time at 317.58 mph (275.97 knots or 511.11 km/h) on Blowering Dam Lake, New South Wales, Australia. The Magic 300 Mark has been exceeded twice by Ken and once fatally by Donald Campbell in 1967.

Ken Warby reached a peak speed of 344.86 mph (555 km/h or 300 knots) unofficially at the same location on 20th November 1977, whilst setting his first water speed record of 288, 60 mph/464.45 km/h,

Spirit of Australia II

Ken and David.

Spirit of Australia II.

The World Water Speed Record is one of great speed challenges in history. I grew up in an environment where boat building was continuous in the backyard; most weekends were spent at race boat meetings around Australia and I was lucky enough to get up close to the boats, racers, sounds and smells. The atmosphere of powerboat racing was something I soaked up from a young age and thoroughly enjoyed.

My father Ken Warby was a champion boat racer builder before I was born; when I was 4 he started to build, in the backyard at home, Spirit of Australia to challenge for the World Water Speed Record. With three J-34 jet engines lying around, tools, timber etc., there was no other place I'd rather have been but down in that backyard next to Dad, seeing what he was doing and helping if I could. This was when I learnt: if you want something bad enough, you can make it happen.

As a young boy I knew all the names of the legends in World Water Speed Record-breaking long before I knew other sportsmen such as Australian football or cricket players' names ... household conversation was always around previous water speed record breakers, the names of their boats, speeds achieved and the stories behind these great men. My father always admired Donald Campbell, as he was the inspiration for his own World Water Speed Record bid.

Most kids want to do what their fathers do; for me watching my father take on the world with very limited resources from the backyard at home and take two World Water Speed Records, realising his lifelong dream, was a huge inspiration. I knew this was the path I would follow: it was part of my DNA. Dad is my mentor and hero.

As a teenager I raced go karts and motorbikes. In my 20s on my own accord I started building and racing hydroplanes in Australia. Dad was living in America still racing jet cars at the time, but as my boats got bigger, faster and my driving experience grew over the years, Dad knew my path to a World Water Speed Record was serious, not a just 5-day wonder; at no stage did Dad ever pressure me to take on boat racing, or the World Water Speed Record. He is very supportive.

In 2011 we discussed building Spirit of Australia II, and in 2012 started construction. It has really been a dream come true to build a boat with Dad. We talk about water speed records as we build and design and talk about what works and what doesn't, as he is the only man ever to design, build and drive a boat to a world record; sometimes I step back and think it's absolutely amazing the current World Water Speed Record-holder, the only man on the planet alive that has held the World Water Speed Record, is next to me to build a boat to take his own record.

Sadly nowadays World Water Speed Record attempts are far and few between. The current record was set in 1978, and the last official challenge made in 1989 by Craig Arfons with fatal results. I believe we have the right design, boat and team to succeed with our challenge.

As soon testing will start with Spirit of Australia II, I feel extremely honoured to enter the arena and take on the a challenge which for me is the Holy Grail of speed records, and tread the path of the legends of the sport; Henry Seagrave, John Cobb, both Campbells, father and son, and my dad Ken Warby; they all realised that sometimes elusive but magical goal of being the fastest on water.

David Warby
Water Speed Record Challenger

Campbell-Norris 7

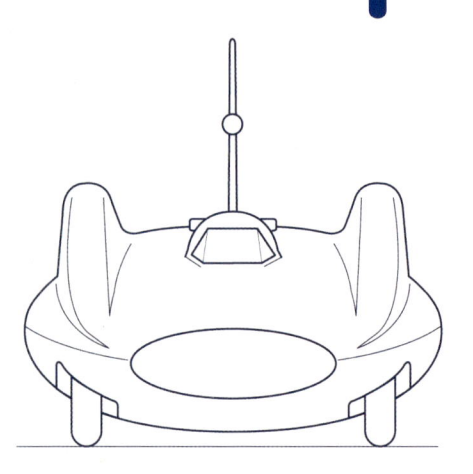

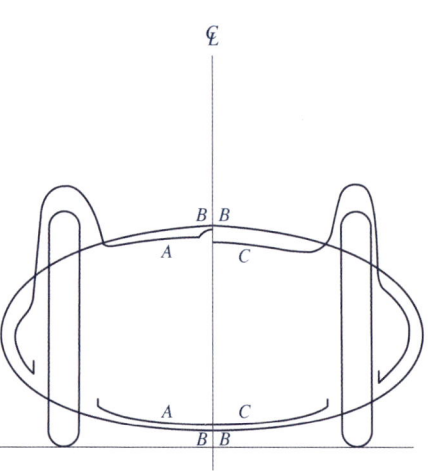

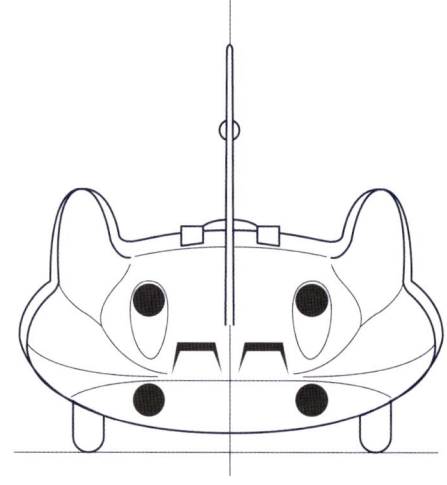

Aerodynamics

Bluebird CN7's shape was dictated by tyre design and the need for neutral aerodynamics: no negative down-force or positive lift. This provides a drag coefficient (cross-sectional area) of only 0.16. Drag at high speed is equal to 30% of the all-up weight, i.e. 1.25 tons. Wind tunnel testing led to an ellipsoidal body with a short straight section in the centre and a 20% camber.

Right-side rear wheel well showing one of the fuel tanks, the engine bay and two of the Proteus' four exhaust ports.

Donald Campbell and Leo in the wind tunnel at Imperial College, London.

204

Araldite

The main frame is an egg-box construction resembling an aircraft frame assembly. The main members and bulkheads are made of honeycomb aluminium alloy sandwich panels (bonded together with Araldite and riveted) providing immense strength and stiffness. The centre of the body is occupied by the Proteus engine with the side bays forming very stiff torsion boxes; access to the fuel tanks is through the wheel wells.

Proteus

Initially powered by a 4,100 bhp modified Bristol-Siddeley 705 Proteus free turbine engine with a drive shaft running straight through linking the forward and rear fixed-ratio, high-speed gearboxes which in turn are connected to the final drives to the wheels. Two sets of gears were built, one for speeds to 400 mph and another for speeds up to 600 mph. The Proteus was a two-spool, reverse-flow gas turbine and because the turbine stages of the inner spool drove no compressor stages and only the drive shaft. It powered the Bristol Britannia airliner, small naval patrol craft, hovercraft and electricity generators.

Braking

On each side of the final drive are mounted disc brakes. The energy of the car at speed is 75 x 10 ft lb, and to bring it to rest in 1 minute (corresponding to 0.3g) involves degrading work to heat at over 2,000 hp. Dissipating this power into the atmosphere at high speed is not feasible, but as the car would be undertaking single runs there was no objection to the energy being retained on board. At high speed the drag of a streamlined vehicle is a highly effective brake and two drag laps were fitted to the rear wings and were expected to add approximately 25% to the wind resistance. The car was also fitted with a parachute.

Systems and controls

Bluebird is controlled by a foot throttle, foot brake and a steering wheel. It has three independent breaking systems, all-round disc brakes operated by compressed air. An emergency system with an entirely different actuating system of high-pressure cylinders is used for the hand-brake for start-up and for demonstration runs.

Instruments

Driving the car is by no means straightforward. The driver has an armoured glass panel in front of his eyes and onto this is projected the display of a Kelvin Hughes accelerometer. This is a demand instrument, the display showing a scale with two indices: one denoting the required and the other denoting the actual acceleration.

The serviceability instruments, the speedometer and galvanometer showing suspension deflection (providing information that was not available when the suspension was designed as to how truly flat the surface is) are filmed by a camera. Since the film cannot be developed in the field, a system of radio telemetry allows the instruments to be monitored on the track side by the crew and in this way the driver can also be informed of any abnormalities during a run.

The conventional cockpit panel has all the instruments needed to check on the serviceability of the vehicle: revolutions, jet-pipe temperature, hydraulic systems, brakes, etc. The driver wears a mask and breathes air from a bottle which overcomes the problems of ventilating the cockpit and preventing the glass and Perspex from steaming up.

Railton

Suspension is not an issue for a car operating on salt flats, since the surface is prepared and effectively plane. A problem that arose was the selection of a design case that would prevent the car from being unrealistically flimsy and the test adopted was proposed by Mr Reid Railton that 'the vehicle should withstand being dropped six inches'. Hard suspension is desirable to minimise torque from the car rolling when accelerating or braking. A vertical movement of 2 inches is provided by independent suspension, using wishbones and oleo-pneumatic spring and damper units.

The cockpit and engine bay can be seen clearly in the centre.

52-inch rubber tyres

Dunlop has developed 41-inch-diameter wheel hubs for extra high speed which were designed to withstand the car rolling over onto to its side. The size of the wheels also gives enough ground clearance for the Proteus engine, the ability to run with one flat tyre and if the vehicle turns over to completely support the top. The 7 x 52 inch pressurised tyres consist of four plies of Fortisan rayon cord with an outer coating of natural rubber of 0.02 inches.

Chronocinégines

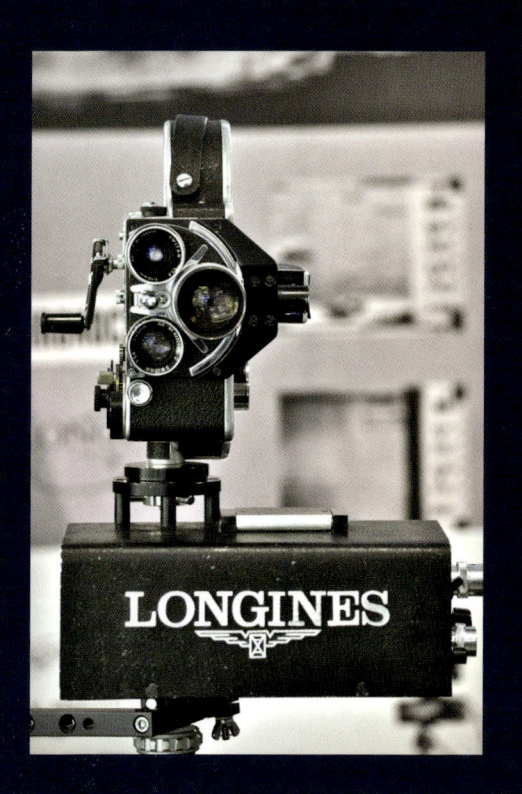

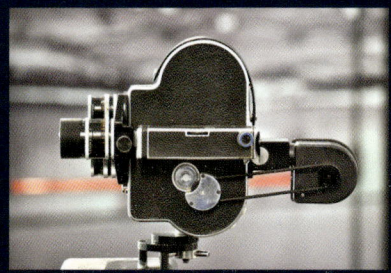

The Longines Chronocinégines was being used by Donald Campbell for his timings from 1956; this instrument united the features of the 16 mm film camera and a high precision timer down to a hundredth of a second working off a 12-volt battery.

Invented in 1954 by Longines, the Chronocinégines is controlled by a quartz-clock (with crystal oscillations of 190,000 per second), ensuring a precision of 10-. The clock's accuracy is attested by an official certificate from the Neuchatel observatory in Switzerland. The camera is a modified Paillard 16 mm Bolex and depending on the event different lenses and film speeds may be used (25, 50 or 100 images per second). The exposed film moves into an interchangeable magazine and 25 seconds after exposure the film is developed and ready for viewing (a magazine contained 30 metres). While the film is being exposed the digits of the time-counter are projected optically onto the film with the digits appearing in the right-hand part of the picture in minutes, seconds and 100th of a second. The value of the photo-finish film was appreciated by judges and press, providing enlargements of up to 50 x 50 cm.

Unlimited Brothers Norris

Donald Stevens & Mike Pepper

Lewis Hunt Norris was born on 20th September 1924, youngest of six sons and two daughters, children of the engineer in charge of the gasworks at Burgess Hill, Sussex. Four of the Norris brothers became qualified engineers, Eric an accountant, and one was killed in the Battle of Britain. Following Lewes Grammar School and West Ham Technical College, Lewis served his apprenticeship with Harland and Wolff at the London docks shipyard, building landing craft for D-Day. Post-war he worked for Burma Oil before joining Kiné engineering, initially owned by his two brother-in-laws, the Meldrum brothers, and Donald Campbell, the managing director.

Kenneth William Norris was born in 1921 and the only one in the family not to go to grammar school. In 1945, at the age of 23, Ken had been apprenticed to the Armstrong Whitworth Aircraft Company at Whitley. He went on to manage the mechanical testing department, while also teaching at Coventry Technical College.

Ken moved on, and enrolled at Imperial College, London, as a full-time student and studied aeronautical engineering. In his spare time he took a course in business administration at the London School of Economics whilst Lew was working on K4 and Ken got involved with Frank and Stella Hanning-Lee, and their White Hawk jet hydrofoil.

They only really had an outline, drawn in chalk on a basement wall, he recalled. 'And I realised that I was going to have to do the whole shooting match. I was virtually imprisoned in this tiny, dark little room, drawing away, until it eventually dawned on me that there wasn't going to be any payment.'

It was whilst at Imperial College that Ken decided he wanted to establish a design consultancy with his brothers. Norris Brothers Ltd was formed in 1954 and by the 1960s it had grown to be one of the most successful, diverse and innovative British design companies of its kind; their work was at the forefront of technology and many of their techniques and inventions are still employed today.

The seat belt, the honeycomb sandwich used in the construction of CN7, is the basis of the crash-protection shell used in Formula 1 today, with modern, stronger and lighter 21st-century materials, air-supported buildings (homes to many tennis/sports clubs), rotary motorcycle engine, a concrete pump, amphibian craft, hydrofoils, racing cars with wings, go karts, confectionery production lines and underground coal gasification plants to name but a few.

Donald Stevens recalls that not a month went by without a visit from Raymond Baxter and BBC TV's *Tomorrow's World* production crew. In fact years later when I interviewed Ken next to CN7 at Beaulieu with Raymond Baxter, they spent the entire morning going over old times together.

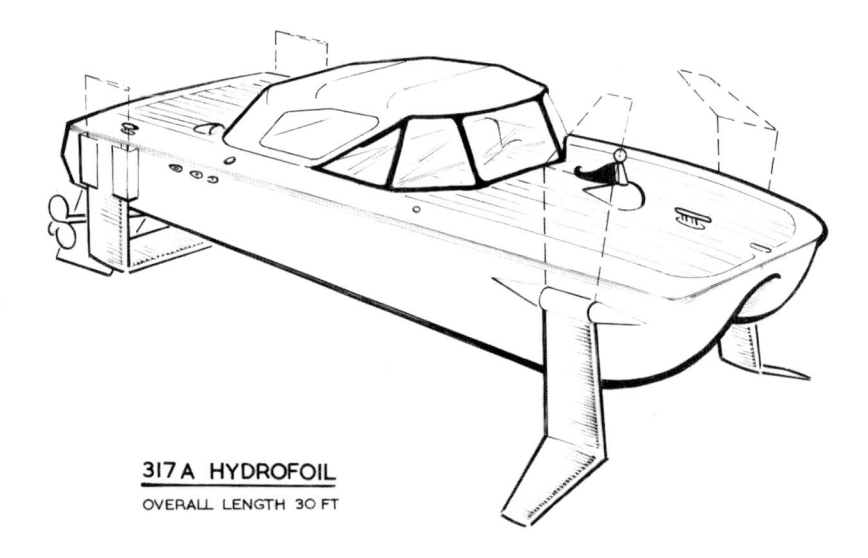

317 A HYDROFOIL
OVERALL LENGTH 30 FT

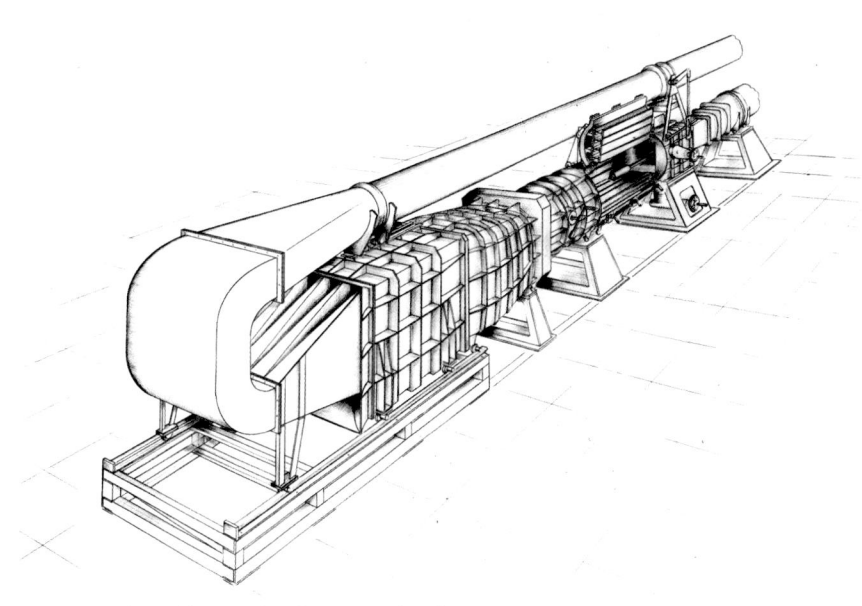

Transonic wind tunnel for research and experimental work.

Even today Worcester UK remains a market leader; its great innovation was the introduction of an advanced management and computer system by Lew long before they became commonplace in business and industry. Subsequently Lew developed and patented the Flotronic pump, renowned for its ease of maintenance in process industries and setup other companies that designed and produced spool valves, packaging machinery, lift trucks and explosion-proof boxes.

Lew eventually moved to the Channel Islands, piloting his twin-engined aircraft to Shoreham from time to time into his 70s. Ken later moved into aviation, qualifying for his private pilot's licence, and set up Anglo-American Airmotive at Bournemouth Airport, a jet engine maintenance and repair facility, a pilot training school in the adjacent flying club and Piper aircraft agencies in the UK and Spain.

The Ford Prefect car for which main assembly fixtures were designed.

As Norris Brothers design and concept grew, Lew realised that design work alone would never make them millionaires, so while Ken was involved with Donald and Bluebird and the design aspect of the business, Lew attacked the manufacturing side.

The first product was a ball-valve made under agreement with the Worcester Valve Co. of Massachusetts, which was eventually bought out by a major British conglomerate, but not before Lew and his team had developed a control system which Norris Brothers licensed back to Worcester in America. He later became Worcester Valve's vice president.

Part of plant for confectionery manufacture.

15 mph

30 mph

50 mph

70 mph

16-foot Speed Boat Test Model at speeds up to 70 mph.

Ken was project manager on Richard Noble's Thrust 2 team during his attempts on the land speed record in the Black Rock desert in Nevada in 1982, and again in 1983, when Noble raised the record to 633.468 mph (1015 km/h). Ken then went on to be design consultant on Richard Noble's Thrust SSC (Super Sonic Car) project, which took the record beyond the sound barrier on land on 15th October 1997, when it achieved a speed of 763 mph (1,228 km/h) with Andy Green at the controls.

Despite their major contribution to British design and engineering, neither Norris brother was honored by his country. Ken Norris died on 1st October 2005. Lew Norris died on 13th February 2009.

My friend Ken Norris

Ken was like a second father to me, but then again, he was like that to a lot of people. Generous to a fault, with his time, his knowledge and experience, there simply wasn't a bad side to him.

I first wrote to Norris Bros in 1973; as a 13 year old schoolboy I had become hooked on the legend of the Blue Birds after my father's death in January 1967, days after Donald Campbell's fatal accident on Coniston Water. Years later, my somewhat unusual hobby became the foundation of a school project, and that is when I wrote to Norris Bros.

I expected a letter signed by a secretary with maybe a picture or a drawing. What I got was a reply from Ken Norris, inviting me to Haywards Heath, and Norris Bros offices. I was treated as no mere visitor: I had a full guided tour, tea, biscuits, and Mr Norris himself giving me the full story. It was when I asked about him that I started to see the real Ken Norris. It meant the world that a man I had only read about in books, was telling me his story, himself, and not once did he treat me as just a schoolboy.

Me? Oh I'm just one of the backroom boys, not very important at all.

He told me how, after Lew's work with Donald Campbell on Blue Bird K4, at a New Year's eve party at Campbell's house, Donald had approached them both with an idea.

'We had a bit of a romp, had the music on, laughed around a bit, and then Donald said to Lew and me, 'Now that you're together, how about designing me a boat?' The rest, as is oft said, is history.'

In later years Ken proved his stature as the ideal project manager, with Richard Noble's Thrust 2 team during his attempts at the Black Rock Desert in Nevada in 1982, and again in 1983. It was after this I became reacquainted with him. He treated me like I had never been away. He refused to shorten my name, and I myself could not bring myself to call him anything other than, Mr Norris. It took me years of nagging on his part for me to call him, simply, Ken.

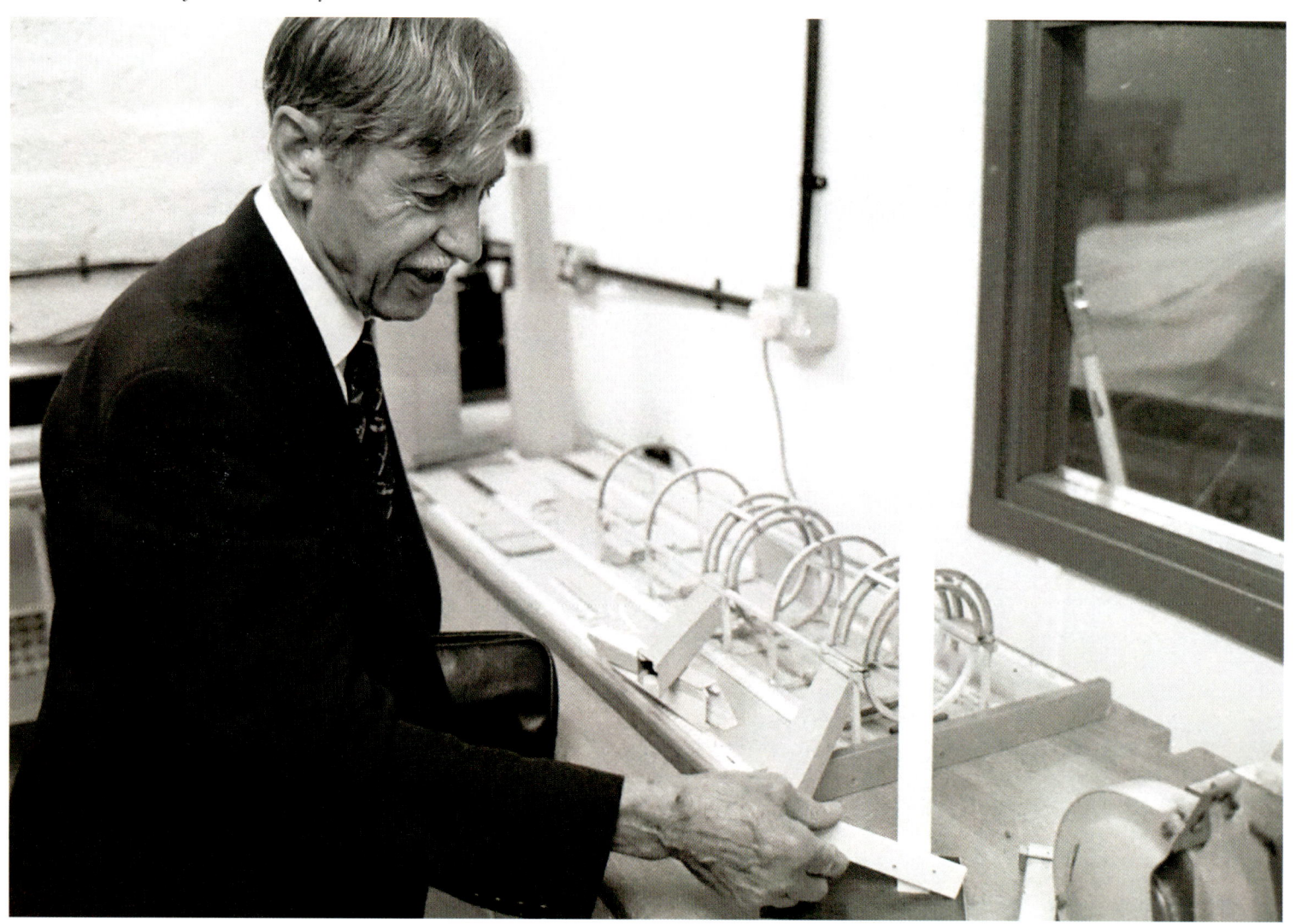

Ken in his element. The project room at Anglo-American with a model of the proposed space frame for Nigel McKnight's Water Speed contender, Quicksilver.

Thrust 2.

Thrust SSC.

Lew and Ken Norris.

The two Kens. Ken Norris and Ken Reakes going over the read-outs from CN7's recorder.

After this second meeting, he would telephone me regularly, send information, and then ask me for advice on subjects he felt I might have a better grasp of. I learnt that he could take little pieces of other people's thinking and assemble them into one working concept, and would then still credit others with it. He had humility in spades, and in the same way that he was so generous with his time and knowledge, he would, much to my pride, also take the time, and say, 'that is some very good thinking there Steven. Would you mind if I take that on and develop it?'

I suppose in the years I knew Ken, we became friends because he was just so easy to get on with, to the point where it was easy to become blasé, even, eventually, when he would ask for my help on things. Until, that is, when K7 and her pilot were finally recovered from Coniston in 2001. As soon as I took the call I knew it had affected Ken more deeply than he wanted anyone to know and there was a fire in his voice that had slowly been going out over the years.

'Steven, there's going to be an inquest, and I need your help.' For the first time I felt I was working alongside Ken Norris. He was, nearly, his old self, full of purpose. I got to see him at work, in his element, slide rule and pad constantly in his hand. Age was his enemy at this time, and it was obvious he was struggling with his memory, but it did not diminish his resolve to get to the facts. It was humbling experience for me.

Ken was a driving force – a force of nature.

So much was achieved simply because Ken Norris was involved.

Steven Holter, 2016

Jetstar

Whilst we were on holiday in the South of France we saw a woman being cut up by a speed boat and from that moment on it was Donald's intention to design a safe water-jet boat, which became the Jetstar project.

Tonia

In August 1966 Donald successfully towed four skiers on a small lake in Knokke in Belgium with the Jetstar prototype perfected by him and Leo and built at Norris Brothers. It was used as a support craft on the final attempt. Following Donald's death, Norris Brothers, Leo Villa and Peter Milne, the designer and magazine editor, continued the commercial development of a water-jet-powered ski boat called Jetstar. It had impressed Mr Kilgour, who had the idea of establishing a factory in Malta's dry docks to eventually turn out 5,000 units a year.

The Dowty craft experience

We had a big family holiday with all the kids out in Majorca on a boat that Donald had rented; he had three of the Dowty jet-boats with him and we had great fun driving them up on beaches. I don't think Donald was very much use to Dowty Marine: even though he was a director he never ever went to the place, but he did get his boats built. I must say they were very good until they got clogged up with seaweed.

We eventually arrived at Palmas and there was a big five-star hotel there with a private beach and Donald got us put up. We carried on driving these boats up onto the private beach and we got into trouble at the posh hotel for frightening the life out of everybody. We went on doing this for a while and eventually we walked into the hotel and the manager threw us out. Donald said to him, 'Don't you know who I am? I'm Donald Campbell!' The manager said he didn't give a f*** if he was Stirling Moss, he'd been messing up his beach all day and he wanted him *out*! First time I'd ever known Donald to be lost for words.

The American fleet

The sixth fleet was in and Donald was driving the boats round and round their aircraft carrier. He got hold of a big melon and went alongside the aircraft carrier and left it. They all thought it was a mine and he got in an awful lot of trouble for that.

Bill Coley

A big boat for the man who likes to feel real power at his finger tips. Seventeen feet of sleek thoroughbred with a beefy six cylinder engine growling at the stern. Built and finished to exacting standards the 525 is an aristocrat of its kind, with room for five or six people in elegant comfort. The list of standard equipment includes many items normally only available as extras on similar boats. Rear bench seat squab folds up to extend upholstered sun deck to 27 square feet.

One man and his dream – 50 years on
Dumbleyung, Western Australia and Donald Campbell

The arrival of Donald Campbell and the Bluebird to the small wheat belt town of Dumbleyung in 1964 caused a major upheaval and contact with the outside world in a way that had not been seen before, bringing the communities of Dumbleyung and Wagin together. Donald Campbell and Bluebird put Dumbleyung Lake into history and it became part of the folklore of the town.

Since then for those who were there and for those who visited in 1964, it has been a source of pride and interest that the World Water Speed Record was broken in our state, on our lake, in a small country town, and it is always mentioned that Donald Campbell only just won the Double that he was trying so hard to achieve.

Over the years there have been many attempts to give due recognition to Donald Campbell and his achievement. On the 20th anniversary of the World Water Speed Record on Lake Dumbleyung, a memorial was designed and built on Pussycat Hill, overlooking the lake. This memorial was unveiled by Gina Campbell, and a celebration event was held.

With the 50th anniversary of Donald Campbell's achievement approaching, members of the community had the concept of building a full-scale replica of the Bluebird to be displayed in the town of Dumbleyung. It took several years of planning, and as the event approached, the Shire of Dumbleyung along with very generous support from local residents raised the necessary funds to enable the Bluebird replica to be built.

A celebratory event was held on New Year's Eve 2014 to commemorate the 50th anniversary of Donald Campbell's World Water Speed Record achievement and to welcome the replica to the town.

June 2016 – a shelter is nearing completion to house the Bluebird replica and an interpretative display has been established in the community resource centre, which has established a worthy memorial for the future.

In a world that has become a global village, having the Bluebird replica and the Donald Campbell story as part of Dumbleyung's history is a valuable asset. Whether it be as a tourist attraction providing jobs and income for the town or teaching future generations about history and human endeavour, it is with pride and a sense of 'it belongs to us' that Dumbleyung considers itself a part of the Donald Campbell speed story.

Christine Bairstow, 2016

What the locals say

As a 16 year old I was aware of the importance of the speed attempt, the lasting image of the Bluebird on the mirror-still lake and echo of the jet engine are with me now all these years later. I think Tonia was a huge asset as she brought glamour to the event and consequently Donald received more cooperation from the local blokes than he might have otherwise had. As a legacy it seems the more time passes the more important history becomes: he put us on the map and we need to honour that fact.

Rodney Frost – local farmer

Donald Campbell's World Water Speed Record in Bluebird in 1964 brought together an unlikely crew of Aussies and Brits to challenge the limits of man and machine to a glorious end. Dumbleyung is internationally recognised now as the location of Donald's last record, a point of pride for our small agricultural community and the greater state of Western Australia. The completed replica and interpretive centre will ensure the Bluebird story is celebrated and shared for many more years to come.

Louisa Dare – farmer, married into the district

The awe of the British speed ace coming to Dumbleyung and mixing with ordinary people. Our parents were involved in providing equipment and voluntary help.

Philip Bairstow – farmer, aged 12 in 1964

I remember the whole school going across the road to the police station to see the Bluebird on the back of a truck when it arrived in town, and visits to the lake to see the Bluebird runs.

Christine Bairstow – farmer, aged 9 in 1964

Bill Caddy and Angus Tuck in 2014 in that same rowing boat left to rot by the lake. They have donated it to the Ruskin Museum.

The replica builders: Mark, Hilary and Jonathan Moitzouris of Statewide Boating.

Peter Carr

The following is a quote from Bryan Cooper, the PR man seconded from BP:

Upon Donald's request Peter Carr and I had arranged a large reception for him in Salt Lake City to coincide with his arrival from New York, for which Peter went to the airport to meet him, whilst I was at the reception to welcome the Governor of the State of Utah, the Mayor of Salt Lake City and other dignitaries. No one was too concerned when, after half an hour, Campbell had not arrived. The plane might have been late, but when an hour went by, we were running out of excuses. It was then that I found, not for the last time, that Campbell was not the easiest of people to deal with. We were just about to ring the airport when Campbell swept in with his wife and casually announced that they had decided to stop off in Las Vegas on the way over, making nonsense of our excuses. It was the kind of dismissive attitude that led to a lot of adverse press comment some years later in Australia. The relationship worsened when Peter asked when he might receive some pay (he had a wife and two children to support) and Donald's response was to hand him a camera with the comment, 'You can sell that old boy.'

On return from Utah, Peter was invited to join BP in their Sales Promotion Team. He went to Lake Eyre on their behalf, but was withdrawn when BP stopped backing the project in 1963.

Peter Carr was a key part of the Bluebird story, yet the role he played is rarely mentioned.

Peter was an RAF Top Gun; his Air Force Cross, which he always maintained he had found in a packet of Cornflakes, was awarded for his exceptional ability, devotion to duty and considerable bravery. He genuinely did not know why he had been awarded the AFC. He also had Letters of Commendation from the UK, Under-Secretary of State and the US Commander of the Combat Crew Training Squadron at Nellis Air Force Base for outstanding devotion to duty, initiative and professional ability. He became Commanding Officer of No. 74 'Tiger' Squadron, a top fighter squadron once commanded by World War II ace 'Sailor' Malan. In 1954 he was posted to the USA as an exchange pilot to evaluate the F-86 Sabre and the F-100 Super Sabre for the RAF. He was also an instructor on the F 100 which was a great honour for a RAF officer given that this was the US Air Force's latest fighter.

It was during his duty at Nellis Air Force Base that he became involved with Donald Campbell and Bluebird. Nellis is 30 miles from Lake Mead and an easy place for Peter to visit, so when K7 was sunk by the wash from careless pleasure boats, he managed to convince his base commander that it would be good US - UK public relations to raise the craft and service it and the Beryl jet engine. Thanks to Peter, exactly one month after the sinking, Donald was able to break the World Water Speed Record for the second time.

Peter was aware that he was to be posted to a desk job at the Air Ministry, a total anathema to a born flyer, and Donald had obviously seen the potential of such a person in his team at Lake Mead and offered him the opportunity to become Director of Operations and reserve driver for CN7, of which I was the project co-ordinator. We worked well together, with Peter in the role of Donald's second in command and me providing the technical back-up. Peter, having led a life in military roles, found Donald's unpredictability difficult to handle, and very frustrating at times; this situation would develop further at Utah, and cause Peter some misgivings over leaving the RAF. Peter's only time in control of CN7 was Run 4 at Goodwood.

Due to Peter's contacts at Nellis AFB, the CN7 team managed to obtain the free use of Hangar 821 at Wendover AFB (the hangar had previously been used by the Enola Gay), a little used satellite to Nellis AFB, which caused some annoyance amongst the US contenders who had to base themselves in local garages or makeshift workshops. Things rather fell apart at Utah.

Bryan Cooper was seconded to the CN7 project by BP, who were major backers. He had previously been to Bonneville in 1957 for MG's class record attempts with their EX-181, so was an ideal addition to the team. Evidently Moss said that 250 mph in the EX-181 seemed more like 500 mph in comparison with a Grand Prix car at 180 mph! Bryan and Peter Carr were the advance party for the CN7 attempt and had to find accommodation for a team of 100 engineers, technicians, press and cameramen. Peter's contact with the USAF was used for CN7's base and storage of 35 tons of spares and equipment. Being just over the border from dry and puritanical Utah, Wendover and nearby towns in Nevada catered for the fun and frolic needs of the citizens of Utah, and, of course, those of the Bluebird entourage! Bryan tells of many riotous times with the 'local ladies', many of whom were there 'for the fun of it' rather than 'professionally'!

Donald Stevens, 2016

Leo Villa OBE

39 Slipshatch Road, Reigate.

'In June 1967 I received an OBE for services to the land and water speed records and was invited to the Palace where I met that dear lady our Queen, she was such a dear and knew all about Donald, the records and all of our exploits. We spoke for quite some time.'

Bill Coley's scrap business in Hounslow, 1977.
'Every time they moved CN7 they called me up.
This time, it was to the National Motor Museum for keeps.'

Leo Villa

1924 — 146.16 mph — 350 HP Sunbeam

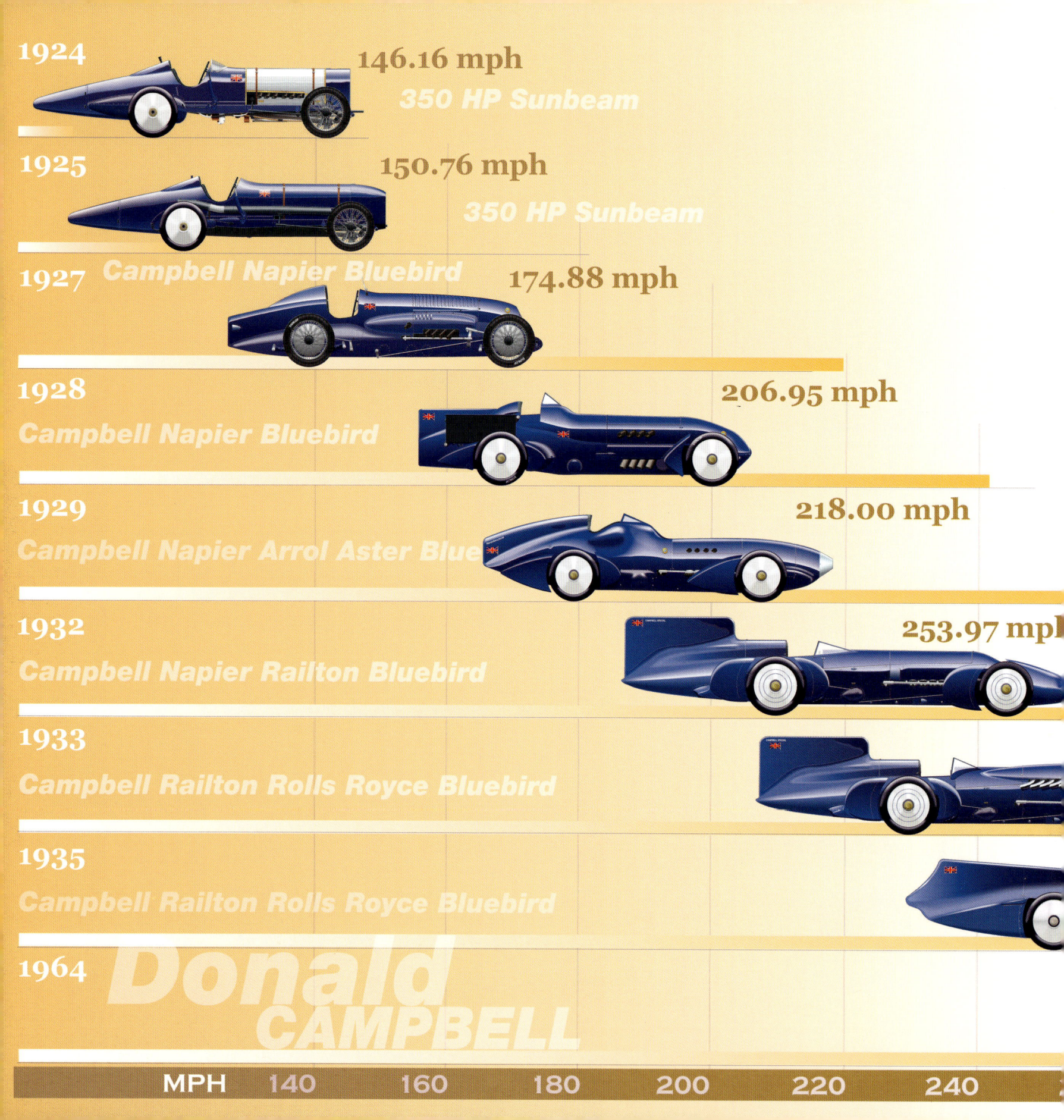

1925 — 150.76 mph — 350 HP Sunbeam

1927 Campbell Napier Bluebird — 174.88 mph

1928 Campbell Napier Bluebird — 206.95 mph

1929 Campbell Napier Arrol Aster Blue — 218.00 mph

1932 Campbell Napier Railton Bluebird — 253.97 mph

1933 Campbell Railton Rolls Royce Bluebird

1935 Campbell Railton Rolls Royce Bluebird

1964 Donald CAMPBELL

| MPH | 140 | 160 | 180 | 200 | 220 | 240 |

FOR THE RECORD

Malcolm CAMPBELL

25TH SEPTEMBER 1924 PENDINE SANDS WALES

21ST JULY 1925 PENDINE SANDS WALES

4TH FEBRUARY 1927 PENDINE SANDS WALES

9TH FEBRUARY 1928 DAYTONA BEACH FLORIDA

25TH APRIL 1929 VERNEUK PARK SOUTH AFRICA
5 AND 10 MILE RECORDS ACHIEVED

5TH FEBRUARY 1931 DAYTONA BEACH FLORIDA 246.09 MPH
24TH FEBRUARY 1932 DAYTONA BEACH FLORIDA

272.46 mph

22ND FEBRUARY 1933 DAYTONA BEACH FLORIDA

301.13 mph

7TH MARCH 1935 BONNEVILLE SALT FLATS UTAH 276.82 MPH
3RD SEPTEMBER 1935 BONNEVILLE SALT FLATS UTAH

Campbell Norris Proteus Bluebird CN7

403.10 mph

17TH JULY 1964 LAKE EYRE AUSTRALIA

280 300 320 340 360 380 400 420

Mick Hill

Malcolm CAMPBELL

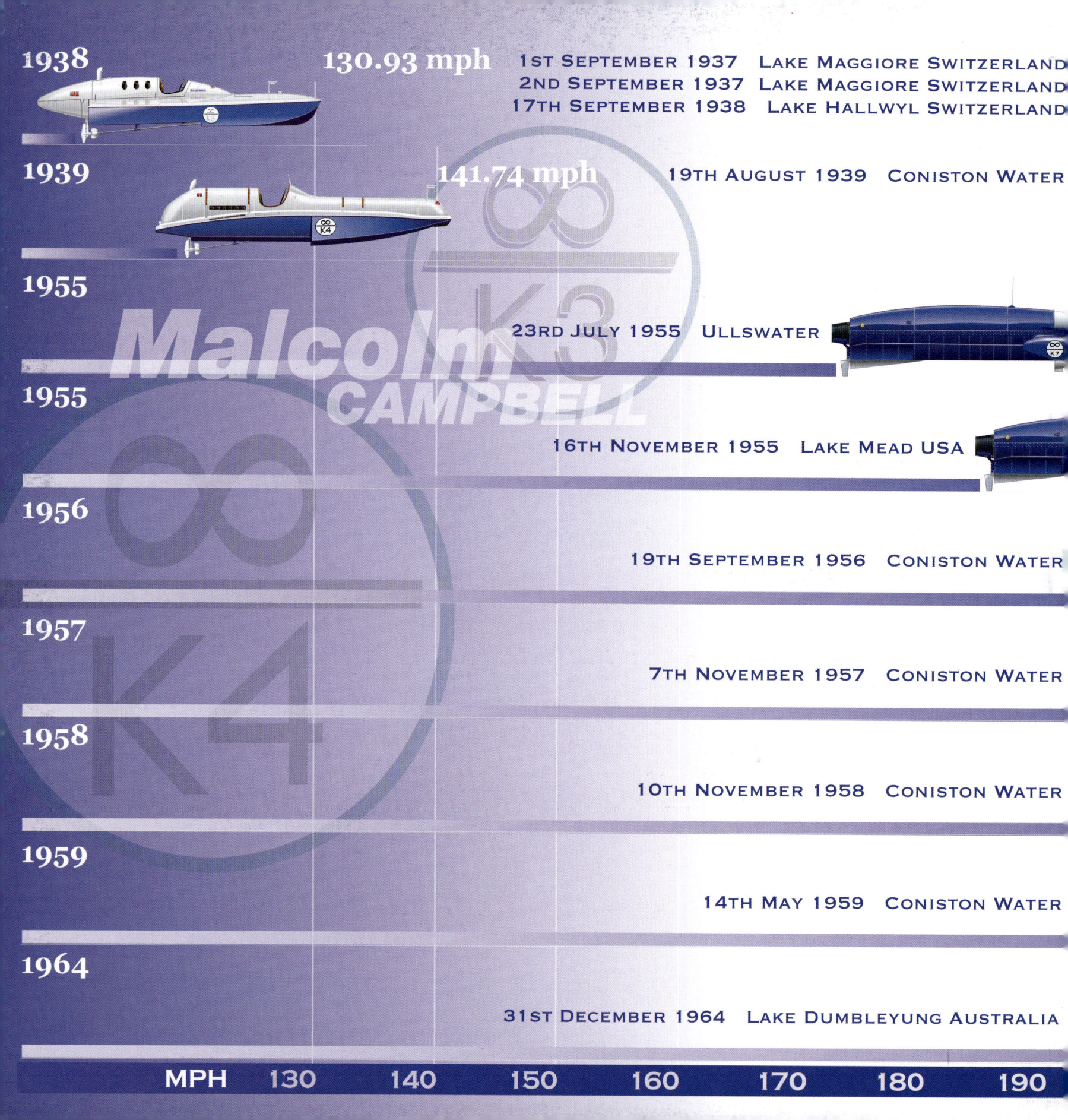

Year	Speed	Date	Location
1938	130.93 mph	1st September 1937	Lake Maggiore Switzerland
		2nd September 1937	Lake Maggiore Switzerland
		17th September 1938	Lake Hallwyl Switzerland
1939	141.74 mph	19th August 1939	Coniston Water
1955		23rd July 1955	Ullswater
1955		16th November 1955	Lake Mead USA
1956		19th September 1956	Coniston Water
1957		7th November 1957	Coniston Water
1958		10th November 1958	Coniston Water
1959		14th May 1959	Coniston Water
1964		31st December 1964	Lake Dumbleyung Australia

MPH 130 140 150 160 170 180 190

FOR THE RECORD

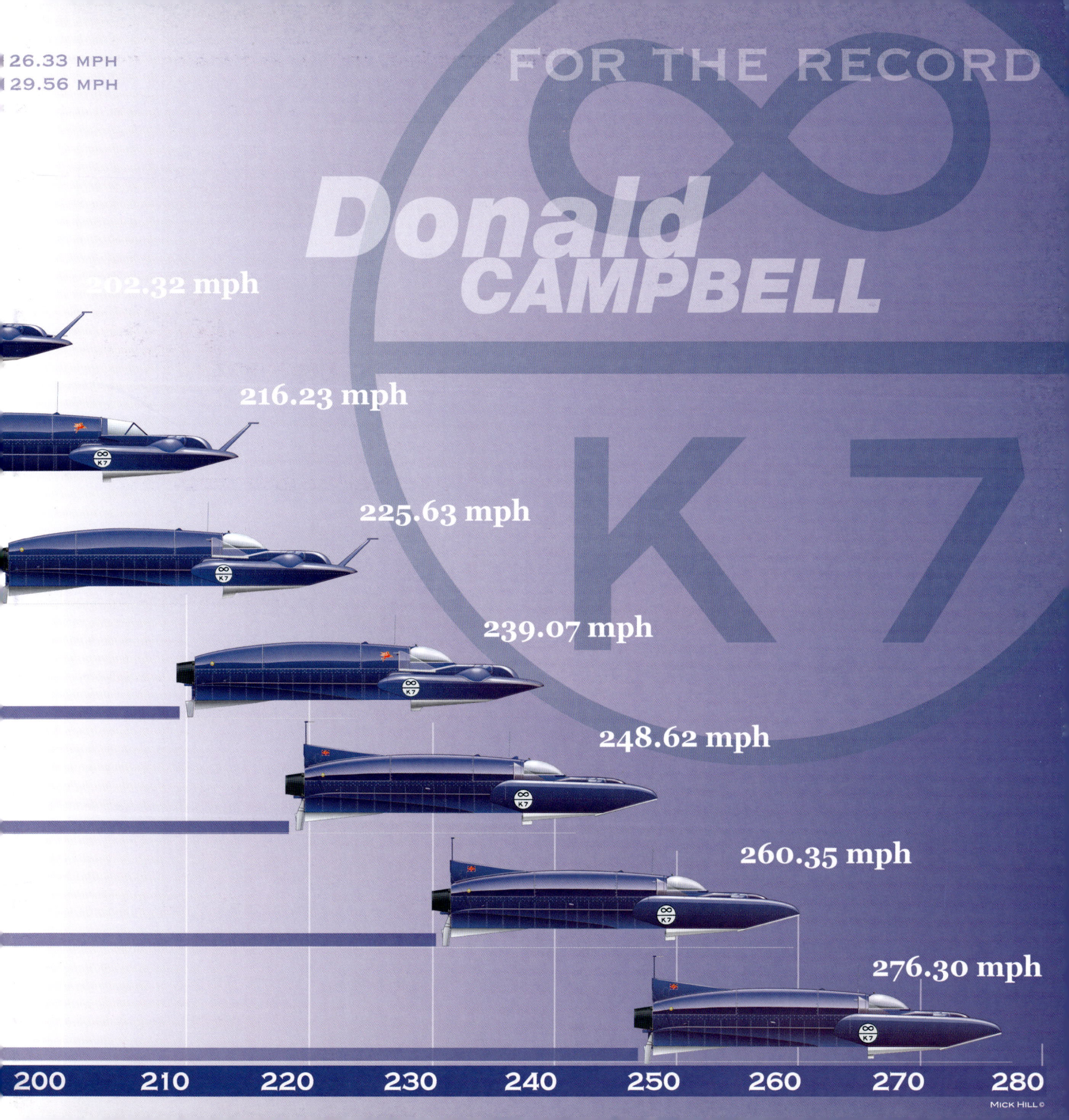

Donald CAMPBELL
K7

26.33 MPH
29.56 MPH

202.32 mph

216.23 mph

225.63 mph

239.07 mph

248.62 mph

260.35 mph

276.30 mph

200   210   220   230   240   250   260   270   280

MICK HILL ©

Index

Adelaide, 156
Barmera, Western Australia, 158
Beryl Jet engine, 68
*Bluebird CN7, specs build, 120
Bluebird CN7, crash Utah, 128
Bluebird CN7, crash rebuild, 132
Bluebird CN7, design team, 122
Bluebird CN8, 174
*Blue Bird K3, 29
Blue Bird K4, 32
Blue Bird K4, Slipper, 33
Bluebird K4, prop-rider, 54
Bluebird K7, specs build, 56, 38, 204
Bluebird K7 1967, cutaway, 178
Bluebird K7, final run, 193
Bluebird LSR table, 188
Bluebird WSR table, 199
Bristol-Siddeley, 177

Butlin, Billy, Sir, 92
Campbell, Gina, 50
Campbell, Sir Malcolm, 12, 13, 14, 20, 23, 26, 28, 32, 36, 48
Campbell, Tonia Bern-, 116
Canandaigua, 1958, 98
Carr, Peter, 84
Coley, Bill, 219
Coniston, 1939, 32
Coniston, 1949-51, 42
Coniston, 1956, 94
Coniston, 1957, 106
Coniston, 1958, 108
Coniston, 1959, 110
Coniston, 1966, 180
Crusader, (Cobb, John), 64, 63
Double, the, 170
Dumbleyung Lake, 162
Dumbleyung Memorial, 220
Eyre, Lake, 1963, 134
Eyre, Lake 1964, 148

Fenn, John, 114
Gardner, Goldie, 36
Geneva Speed Trials 1938, 30
Goodwood, 1960, 122
Hallwill Lake, 1938, 31
Harvey, Daphne, 48
Jet-cars (US), 175
Jetstar, 218
Las Vegas, 80
Little Abbotts, 62
Little Gatton, 36
Longines, 172, 188, 212
Maggiore, Lake, 1937, 29
McKegg, Dorothy, 62
Mead, Lake, 1955, 80
Moss, Stirling, 219
Motor Panels Ltd, 121
Muloorina, 135
Nellis Air Force Base, 84
Norris Brothers Ltd, 214
Norris, Kenneth, 214, 216

Norris, Lewis, 214
Oltranza Cup, 54
Orpheus jet engine, 177
Pendine Sands, 20
Personnel Canandaigua, 99
Povey Cross, 14
Proteus gas turbine engine, 209
Sahara Hotel, 80
Sayers, Stanley, 53
Slo-Mo-Shun IV, 53
Swan River, 168
Ullswater 1955, 72
Utah, 1935, 22
Utah, 1960, CN7 crash, 126
Verneuk Pan, 21
Villa, Leo, 18, 24, 30, 40, 57, 78, 90, 96, 100, 110, 130, 188, 223
Warby, Ken and Dave, 5, 202

*Note: Donald Campbell took over record-breaking from Sir Malcolm in 1949 and changed the spelling of The Blue Bird to Bluebird.

Museums:
Brooklands, Weybridge
Ruskin Museum, Coniston
Lakeland Motor Museum, Lake District
National Motor Museum, Beaulieu
Coventry Transport Museum
Think Tank Museum, Birmingham
Museum of Speed, Pendine Sands
The Science Museum, London

Clubs:
www.speedrecordclub.com
www.bluebirdsupportersclub.com

Books, models, DVDs and memorabilia:
Speed Record Models & Memorabilia
geoff.holden@gofast.co.uk/Facebook

Further reading:
Daughter of Bluebird, Gina Campbell
My Speed King, Tonia Bern-Campbell
Leo Villa's Bluebird Album with 3D images, David de Lara
The Unobtainable – a Story of Blue, book with 80 mins DVD, David de Lara
Leap into Legend, Steve Holter
Bluebird CN7, Donald Stevens
The Final Record Attempt, Neil Sheppard
The Man Behind the Mask, David Tremayne

Films:
Remembering Donald, 80 mins, produced and directed by David de Lara
How Long a Mile, 28 mins, produced and directed by Donald Campbell

Bluebird K7 restoration:
www.bluebirdproject.com